THE POWER OF LETTING

Go

PAM VREDEVELT

Multnomah® Publishers *Sisters, Oregon*

THE POWER OF LETTING GO
published by Multnomah Publishers, Inc.
© 2005 by Pam Vredevelt
International Standard Book Number: 1-59052-598-1
Cover design by Kirk DouPonce, DogEaredDesign.com
Cover photo by Paige Craige-Apodaka, www.pcaphotography.com
Makeup artist: Heidi Nymark, www.celestineagency.com
Hair design by Kristi Gradwahl, Salon Ambiance, Gresham, Oregon
Interior design and typeset by Katherine Lloyd, The DESK

Italics in Scripture are the author's emphasis.
Unless otherwise indicated, Scripture quotations are from:
The Holy Bible, New International Version © 1973, 1984 by International
Bible Society, used by permission of Zondervan Publishing House

Other Scripture quotations are from:
New American Standard Bible® (NASB) © 1960, 1977, 1995
by the Lockman Foundation. Used by permission.
The Holy Bible, New King James Version (NKJV) © 1984 by Thomas Nelson, Inc.
The Holy Bible, King James Version (KJV)
The Living Bible (TLB) © 1971. Used by permission of Tyndale
House Publishers, Inc. All rights reserved.
Holy Bible, New Living Translation (NLT) © 1996.
Used by permission of Tyndale House Publishers, Inc. All rights reserved.
The Message by Eugene H. Peterson © 1993, 1994, 1995, 1996, 2000,
2001, 2002 Used by permission of NavPress Publishing Group
The Amplified Bible (AMP) © 1965, 1987 by Zondervan Publishing House.
Contemporary English Version (CEV) © 1995 by American Bible Society

Multnomah is a trademark of Multnomah Publishers, Inc.,
and is registered in the U.S. Patent and Trademark Office.
The colophon is a trademark of Multnomah Publishers, Inc.
Printed in the United States of America

ALL RIGHTS RESERVED
No part of this publication may be reproduced, stored in a retrieval system,
or transmitted, in any form or by any means—electronic, mechanical, photocopying,
recording, or otherwise—without prior written permission.

For information:
MULTNOMAH PUBLISHERS, INC.
601 N. LARCH STREET • SISTERS, OREGON 97759

Library of Congress Cataloging-in-Publication Data
Vredevelt, Pam W., 1955-
The power of letting go / Pam Vredevelt.
    p. cm.
Includes bibliographical references.
ISBN 1-59052-598-1
1. Peace of mind--Religious aspects--Christianity. 2. Liberty--Religious aspects--
Christianity. I. Title.
BV4908.5.V75 2006
248.4--dc22

                                                          2005029213
06 07 08 09 10—10 9 8 7 6 5 4 3 2 1 0

This book is dedicated to Jessie...
My heart sings when I see you let go
of that which would rob you of God's best
and cling tightly to Him.

CONTENTS

THANK YOU...

*T*hank you, Don Jacobson, for facilitating new beginnings. You graciously encouraged me to follow God's lead into a season of stillness and then rereleased me when God said, "Start writing again." You have had many outstanding successes, but I believe your greatest impact in publishing is yet to come.

Thank you, Kimberly Brock, for your fresh vision. Your creative thinking and enthusiasm for women to realize their God-given freedom and favor inspires me.

Thank you, Bonnie Johnson, for being our team leader. You have been the oil that has kept the wheels turning smoothly and efficiently in spite of the glitches that typically accompany any big project.

Thank you, Jennifer Barrow, for helping me develop this new book. I appreciate the time and energy you invested to help me coach women to a place where they can experience the power of letting go.

Thank you, Larry Libby, for displaying God while doing the painful work of letting go. Those who know you stand in awe of the God who graces you with His Spirit of endurance and hope.

ASK YOURSELF, WHY CAN'T I LET GO?

~

*A day of worry is more exhausting
than a day of work.*

SIR JOHN LUBBOCK

Chapter One

EXPLORE YOUR CORE VALUES

*I*n my counseling office and during my travels as a speaker, I frequently hear these kinds of questions from men and women:

"How can I let go of my disappointment?"

"How do I move on after the death of my dream?"

"How will I ever experience joy after the loss I've suffered?"

"Will I always be tormented by worries, or is there a way to find peace?"

These souls genuinely long for rock-solid answers in the midst of the conflicts and harsh realities of their lives.

During the last several years I've asked more than one thousand people this question: What are you finding difficult to let go of at this time in your life? Here's what many of them said:

I am finding it hard to let go of...

...a friendship that went sour.

...a job I loved and lost to corporate change.

...my teenager who has gone astray.

...my shameful past.

...my spouse of fifty-two years.

...my reputation after I made a terrible mistake.

...my childhood dreams, which aren't realistic anymore.

...my son/daughter who recently married and moved away.

...my stillborn baby.

...my keepsakes that were lost in a fire.

...my expectations that things would turn out the way I wanted.

...my health.

In every season of life we are faced with disappointments, anxiety, anger, and other disturbing emotions that we must learn to let go of for our own good. Letting go, however, requires us to confront many of the core values of our culture.

People today value competence, achievement, gain, accumulation, control, self-sufficiency, and independence. Capitalizing on our fear of losing these things, advertisers hit us from a thousand different angles, prodding and urging us to seek more "stuff" in order to feel satisfied. You've heard the messages over and over again. They say that the more you have, the more valued, powerful, sexy, and successful you will be. Of course, the flip side of that message is: "The less you have, the less valued, powerful, sexy, and successful you will be."

It's a deceptive, toxic thesis that sets us up for disappointment and undermines our sense of contentment. Although our culture conditions us to accumulate and hang on, peace and true satisfaction come with letting go.

Cheryl, a woman who came to me for counseling, told me that before she had quadruple bypass heart surgery, she experienced a pervasive feeling of emptiness. "I bought bigger houses and nicer cars, filled more closets with clothes, and redecorated every year. I wanted more, more, more to fill the hole inside. I kept thinking, *If I just have more, the emptiness will go away.*"

But Cheryl's heart attack and subsequent surgery changed things. Life-threatening situations typically do. In preparation for her hospital stay, she packed a small, dark green suitcase with a few personal belongings. All the items fit neatly in her compact canvas bag-on-wheels. During her recovery she used the same robe, the same slippers, the same comb, and the same brush every day. She read from one of the two books that she had brought with her, selected from her library of hundreds.

One afternoon, Cheryl was surprised by the contentment she felt. "I was rummaging through my suitcase, which contained five or six items from home," she said, "and it dawned on me that the emptiness was gone. The surgery had gone well. The prognosis was good. God had granted me life. I had everything I needed."

A month later, Cheryl and a friend held a three-day garage sale at which she sold much of what she had accumulated over the years. "More isn't necessarily better," she concluded. "When I let go of all that stuff, I let go of the illusions that came with it."

Cheryl's physical illness had facilitated emotional healing. The heart surgery had been successful on two counts: It had given her another chance to live, and it had helped her release her grip on the clutter that was holding her hostage.

How about you? Are you hanging on to anything that might be holding you hostage? Are you feeling stuck and frustrated because where you are is *not* where you want to be? Are you tightfisted with anything that might be blocking you from emotional freedom and peace?

One evening, at a large women's conference where I was speaking, I heard comments like:

"I'm in a really good place right now, but I keep wondering when the other shoe is going to drop."

"My kids are having a great year—knock on wood—but I don't know how long that's going to last."

"Things are going well. But I worry about being too happy because I don't want to be disappointed again."

Fear had crept in, and it was blocking these women from enjoying the good times afforded them.

I have yet to meet a person who doesn't feel worried or anxious now and then. It's a prevalent problem in today's frantic, fast-paced, information-overloaded society. Harvard Business Review has reported that stress-related symptoms account for 60 to 90 percent of medical office visits.[1] The media bombard us with ads for products designed to treat such ailments—Tums, Rolaids, Maalox, Excedrin, Tylenol, Advil—and many of us have these products on the shelves in our homes. Pharmaceutical companies spend huge sums of money developing and marketing medications to treat the physical problems resulting from prolonged anxiety. Tagamet, Zantac, Valium, and Xanax are among the most prescribed drugs in America. Some researchers have concluded that anxiety is currently the most damaging disease in America.[2]

In the twenty-five years I've been a therapist, I think I've treated more people suffering from anxiety than from any other problem. This parallels national statistics. Anxiety is the most common complaint to psychotherapists and the fifth most common complaint received by doctors. One out of four Americans is diagnosed with an anxiety disorder during his or her lifetime. One-third of the general population experienced a panic attack in the last year.[3] In short, if you struggle with worry and anxiety, you are not alone.

My interest in this *dis*-ease is far more than professional. I have personally wrestled with it on several levels. It can manifest itself as a simple case of the butterflies before I speak at a large conference. In this case the worry is positive—it triggers just enough adrenaline to allow keen concentration and peak performance. But when anxiety takes a stronger hold and leaves me with racing thoughts, over-amped nerves, a dry mouth, a rapid heartbeat, and "brain freeze," it's anything but positive. It's a real nuisance. How about you?

Are you worried about your marriage?

Are concerns about your children keeping you up at night?

Are fears about the stock market or debt sapping your energy reserves?

Are you anxious about your health? Are fears about death ever present?

Are you fretting over whether you're going to be rejected by the college you want to attend or the person you'd like to date?

Are you obsessing about whether you'll be able to get a new job or hang on to the job you have?

Is your imagination running wild with what ifs?

Don't be surprised. Anxiety and strain are in our very airwaves in this culture. (Just think of all those invisible, high-stress cell phone calls zipping through the atmosphere all around you!) Because we live in a world filled with unpredictable, threatening situations—so often beyond our control—it's virtually impossible to completely eliminate stress. But there are time-tested truths and clinically proven strategies that can greatly increase our peace of mind and our ability to enjoy life. We'll talk about some of these effective tools in this book.

But here's the best news of all: Finding fulfillment and freedom from stress *is not all up to us*. We don't have to pull ourselves up by the bootstraps and make the good stuff happen. God is waiting in the wings, ready to resource us seven days a week, twenty-four hours a day. Are you ready? Are you willing to risk opening some new doors in your heart to God? Are you willing to explore your core values and consider some new ways of thinking?

We all have problems without remedies and questions without answers. We all have holes in our souls. But acknowledging this takes courage, because we don't easily accept and embrace weakness, need, loss, or suffering. For the most part, we harbor a subtle contempt for the weaknesses or deficiencies we perceive in ourselves and others.

And the result? We end up rejecting key parts of our own humanity. We gloss over our needs rather than admit them. We deny, minimize, or at least sidestep many forms of suffering.

That's what gets us stuck! Stuck in our pain. Stuck in our depression. Stuck in our need. We lose forward movement and become victims of our own faulty thinking rather than survivors who experience firsthand the power of letting go and moving on.

In the following pages you'll meet many people who, like you, have struggled to let go. I pulled some of the stories from my personal journals. Others came from people with whom I've had the privilege of crossing paths, people who have taught me about holding things loosely.

Please understand this: The tragedies you have suffered—the troubles you have endured—do not define who you are. Nor do they hold your future hostage. I firmly believe that no matter where you are in life right now, the best is yet to come. Your best years are ahead. Your biggest joys and God's greatest surprises are still up ahead, around the corner, just over the horizon. God is standing in your future, saying, "Come on! Let's go. There's so much for you to look forward to. I've got great plans for you. I know everything you are enduring, and I care. Your worries matter to me. I am with you in your heartache and have not abandoned you. Your pain is not an obstacle to Me. My miracles always begin with a problem."

I firmly believe that the weak and broken places in our souls are the very places where God moves powerfully in divine visitations. He makes this promise: "If you return to me, I will restore you.... I will give you back your health and heal your wounds" (Jeremiah 15:19; 30:17, NLT).

God is on a mission to restore you. He is well aware of the problems, challenges, and heartaches that are an integral part of our human condition. And God is a gentleman. He will not force Himself on anyone. But when we extend an invitation, God delights in releasing His healing power right into the center of our pain. Our wounds don't have to limit us. They can become the springboard that launches us into a deeper understanding of ourselves, a more fulfilling relationship with God, and the joy of being a woman who leaves an eternal mark in this world.

That's what this book is all about: letting go of what doesn't matter and opening your hands to what does.

In the pages ahead I'll nudge you to consider the following questions:

"How can I let go of the life I thought I wanted so I can receive the very best God has for me?"

"What is God's part and what is my part in the equation that leads to freedom?"

"How can I embrace today, release my yesterdays, and prepare for my tomorrows?"

I'll also encourage you to take an honest look at the issues that trigger your frustration and anger and consider how these emotions can be used for good. We'll review helpful strategies for restoring emotional balance when life blindsides you and consider various ways God heals us from the inside out.

Through various sufferings, I have learned that the empty places created by letting go become the places God fills with His richest blessings.

He replaces our weakness with His strength.

He exchanges our confusion for His wisdom.

He takes our anguish and leaves His peace.

As we let go of our self-sufficiency and wildly abandon our hearts to God, His Spirit accomplishes what we cannot. He renews. He refreshes. He restores us. He resurrects the dead places in our souls, and we experience firsthand the healing *power of letting go*.

Reclaim Your Life

FOOD FOR THOUGHT

"You will know the truth, and the truth will set you free."

JOHN 8:32

PRAYER FOR TODAY

Lord, I know these feelings: worry, anxiety, fear. Too often they feel like constant companions. More than anything I want to let go of my anxiety, my fear, my disappointments, my anger, my frustration. I believe that You have wondrous things for me on the other side of letting go. Lord, please help me to step boldly onto the path of letting go that You lay out before me through this book. Thank You for the power to do it. In Jesus' name I pray, amen.

STEPS TO TAKE THIS MONTH

- What values or beliefs are blocking you from letting go? Ask God to reveal them to you, and write them down as you discover each one. Meditate on each of these beliefs and then praise God for the freedom you will experience as He equips you with the power to let go of them.

- Are you ready for the serious work of letting go? If you are, make a commitment today that you will work diligently and seek the Lord persistently throughout this journey. Ask Him to be with you.

EMBRACE TODAY

*A mind that travels to the future or the past
is fertile ground for worry and anxiety.*

Chapter Two

REALIZE WHEN YOU'RE GRASPING

*The reason why many are still troubled, still seeking,
still making little forward progress is because they have not yet
come to the end of themselves. We are still giving some of the orders,
and we are still interfering with God's working within us.*

A. W. TOZER

$\mathcal{B}$illy Graham tells a story about a small boy caught playing with an extremely valuable vase. The little guy had put his hand into the vase but couldn't take it out. His father tried his best to help the boy, but all his efforts were in vain.

They were thinking gloomily of breaking the beautiful vase when the father sighed and said, "Now, son, try one more time. Open your hand and hold your fingers out straight, as you see me doing, and then pull."

To his dad's astonishment the little fellow said, "Oh no, Father. I couldn't put my fingers out like that. If I did, I'd drop my penny!"[4]

Smile if you will, but, truth be told, you and I are a lot like that little boy—so busy holding on to what we should be letting go of that we cannot accept freedom.

When Carl came to see me, his wife had just told him that she had found a lover and no longer wanted to be married. Looking at the floor and shaking his head in utter disbelief, he said, "I know I have my faults, but divorce? I just never thought it would come to this." As far as his wife was concerned, the relationship was over, and Carl wanted help in adjusting to the many losses that accompanied the divorce. At sixty-four he thought that starting over was an impossible task.

During the months that followed, Carl and Nancy divided their assets, signed papers, and committed to parting amicably. Carl moved out, purchased another home, and tried to begin a new life. After the divorce was finalized, he dated off and on but continued to call Nancy on a regular basis. Whenever he came into my office after seeing her, Carl was in a downward spiral.

Hanging on was killing him.

Choosing my words carefully, I commented on the obvious pattern. But Carl wasn't ready to think about severing the connection.

Then, on the night of his sixty-fifth birthday, an interesting turn of events seemed to propel Carl forward in his healing. He invited a group of friends, including Nancy, over for dessert. After everyone else left, he and Nancy spent some quiet moments alone, reminiscing about old times. That night Carl went to bed feeling rather morose, and he had a series of distressing dreams with a repetitive theme. "In each dream I was lost," he said, "trying to find my way, unsuccessfully groping in the darkness for something to hang on to. I kept banging into things and getting hurt."

The following morning, Carl worked on some projects in his garage for a couple of hours. Shaking his head in exasperation, he said, "I was all fingers. It was as if everything I reached for was just beyond my grasp. I'd go to pick up a tool, miss it by an inch, and slam my hand into something else." The red marks on his knuckles told the story.

Carl was insightful, and I wondered aloud if he saw the thread woven throughout the incidents he had just described. He pondered the question, but nothing seemed to surface.

I offered a suggestion: "Could those dreams and your experience in the garage the next morning be expressions of the conflict you feel from trying to hang on to Nancy?"

Light dawned. After a few moments of quiet thought, he looked at me and said, "Yeah. I believe that about hits the nail on the head."

The session ended shortly thereafter, and a month later Carl scheduled another appointment with me. This time he looked rested and stood an inch taller. I sensed his grief, but I also detected less agitation and a more forward focus. I commented on this and asked if he could identify what had made the difference.

He said, "I've quit grasping."

If we want to move successfully from one season of life to the next, at times we will have to release our grip on things we naturally want to hang on to. And when we do, we must expect at first to experience intense and complex emotions. As endings, empty spaces, rifts, separations, and little deaths come our way, so do feelings of grief. When we are grieving such losses, it helps to know that God has good counsel for us. He hasn't left us hanging. Solomon penned these lovely lines, which are so much more than poetry:

> There is a time for everything,
> and a season for every activity under heaven:
> a time to be born and a time to die,
> a time to plant and a time to uproot,
> a time to kill and a time to heal,
> a time to tear down and a time to build,
> a time to weep and a time to laugh,
> a time to mourn and a time to dance,
> a time to scatter stones and a time to gather them,

a time to embrace and a time to refrain,
a time to search and a time to give up,
a time to keep and a time to throw away,
a time to tear and a time to mend,
a time to be silent and a time to speak,
a time to love and a time to hate,
a time for war and a time for peace....
{God} has made everything beautiful in its time.
He has also set eternity in the hearts of men.
(Ecclesiastes 3:1–8, 11)

God has made everything beautiful...*in its time*.
Even the empty spaces.
Even the holes.

I admit that it's a hard concept for me to believe when I'm frantically grasping the last few strands of whatever is trying to escape my clutches. The pain involved in letting go doesn't feel "beautiful" to me; it feels downright miserable.

Yet in God's economy, new life springs forth from death. Jesus tried to help His followers understand this. His disciples had seen His triumphs, witnessed His miracles, experienced His power. They thought He was going to establish His kingdom on earth. Then, one afternoon, Jesus sat down on a hillside and told them that the time had come for Him to be glorified, but not in the manner in which they expected. Instead, it was to be by His death. And, with tenderness and feeling, Jesus comforted them with an illustration:

"The time has come for the Son of Man to be glorified. Listen carefully: Unless a grain of wheat is buried in the ground, dead to the world, it is never any more than a grain of wheat. But if it is buried, it sprouts and reproduces itself many times over. In the same way, anyone *who holds on to life* just as it is destroys that life. But if you *let it go,* reckless in your love, you'll have it forever, real and eternal....

"Right now I am storm-tossed. And what am I going to say? 'Father, get me out of this'? No, this is why I came in the first place. I'll say, 'Father, *put your glory on display.*'" (John 12:23-25, 27-28, *The Message*)

Jesus bids us turn our eyes on the fields and observe the mature grain ready for harvest. He explains the process: no loss, no gain; no death, no new life. For Christ the analogy was very personal: His death was to become the very gateway to life! Without His death, there would be no resurrection—for any of us.

The message is for you and me as well. It's a message of hope when life steals from us and leaves us with empty arms. It's a message of strength when we've been stripped bare and feel as though we're facing the future empty-handed. It's a message of substance that can fill the holes in our souls with a promise. God says to us:

When you are letting go,
remember that I am planting seeds of new life in you.
Your grief is only for a season.
My end is not death. It is always life.
I am the author of life.[2]

These are the promises we have to hang on to when we are doing the hard work of letting go.

Did you catch that? Letting go is hard work. It is often very bewildering. To break away from someone or something we have been bonded to rips at our emotions. It goes against our natural instincts. The parting cannot happen without inward bleeding. The greater the bond, the greater the pain.

Our heads and our hearts are usually in conflict. Our heads say, *I need to do this for my own good. I need to let go because it's right. I need to let go because God is telling me to let go. I need to let go for the sake of my kids or my spouse or my friendship or my own growth and development.* But our hearts say, *Oh, no you don't! It hurts too much. I can't do it. I won't do it!* Our logic and our emotions war with each other.

But there are some things we can do to cooperate with God in the process of letting go. We can take certain steps to help us move down life's path with a sense of curiosity and adventure, minus the claw marks. In the next chapters we will look at how we can cooperate with God and experience the power of letting go.

Chapter Three

RECOGNIZE THAT WHAT IS, *IS*

There is no power on earth more formidable than the truth.

MARGARET LEE RUNBECK

*L*etting go is a process.

Please don't fly right past that statement.

You might say, "Well, I already know that." And maybe you do...in your head. But our hearts often lag behind—way behind—our knowledge base.

Letting go is NOT an instantaneous event.

It starts with an awareness of a difficult reality, and as our awareness increases, so does our pain. I once saw a poster that described the process perfectly. It was a cartoon of a woman whose head and arms were being squeezed through the wringers of an old washing machine. Beneath her anguished face the caption read, "The truth will set you free, but first it will make you miserable."

Facing the truth can be very difficult. Like surgery, acknowledging our disappointments and losses may hurt, but it can help move us toward wholeness. If we deny, block, stuff, or numb the pain, we end up camping out in our grief and never progressing beyond it. We cut ourselves off from the treasures God wants to deposit in our empty spaces, and we put our emotions into lockdown.

As a counselor I see this regularly in people like you and me. I'm talking about typical, get-up-in-the-morning-and-go-to-work, raise-the-kids kinds of people. Moms who help with the PTA. Dads who coach Little League. Brothers. Sisters. Aunts. Uncles. Folks who seem normal on the outside but who are locked up on the inside.

Take Marissa for example. Marissa was skilled at keeping secrets—not because she wanted to, but because it was how she had learned to survive. Her father had sexually abused her from the time she was a little girl, and she didn't dare tell anyone. If she did, her father said, he would put her in jail and kill her mother. Little girls believe their big, strong daddies. In Marissa's innocent mind there were no options. She had to be a good little girl. And part of being good was keeping the secret.

But the terrible secret, buried for so many years and landscaped with neat shrubbery and little flowers, became like a hidden toxic waste dump. The poison seeped into the very soil of her life, gradually numbing and warping her soul—even the good parts. I saw evidence of the hidden toxins in her words:

"I want to enjoy my husband and kids, but I have no feelings."

"It's as if I'm numb. Flat. I can't tell the difference between happy and sad."

"Nothing matters to me, even though I want it to matter."

"I used to be passionate and sensitive. I used to care. It's not like me not to care."

Again, we weren't built to bury our feelings alive. We weren't designed to deny our pain or to live by a "no talking" rule. The mind has limitations built into its defense system. If we block the bad, we also block the good.

The result?

No sorrow…but no joy either.

No heartache…but no passion for life.

No grief…but no capacity for laughter.

It all gets locked up together.

The good news is that there are keys to unlocking our pain, and they are right in our pockets. The first key is to recognize that what is, *is*. It is the essence of being brutally honest with ourselves and looking our painful truths in the face.

Sarah is a wonderful example of someone who courageously faced her pain and let it go. She came to our sessions impeccably dressed in the latest vogue, her makeup applied to perfection. But the eyes that stared at me were cold and as hard as chiseled marble. Sarah had struggled with an eating disorder for nearly twenty years, and she was one of the most bitter and controlling people I had ever worked with.

As we talked, I expected to uncover the source of Sarah's bitterness. But the account of her childhood was rather typical and uneventful. No great traumas. No major heartbreaks. Her parents had a good marriage, and she spoke of a close relationship with both them and her two brothers. She butted heads with the boys now and then, as most kids do in the healthiest of families, but there was nothing out of the ordinary. Besides being blessed with parents who loved each other, she had the support of grandparents who lived next door. Her grandmother was like a second mom and confidante to Sarah, especially during her teen years.

As she reviewed her life during that first session, I was puzzled. The family dynamics didn't fit the common profiles of patients with eating disorders. They weren't even close—no divorce, no abuse, no drugs or alcohol. Neither parent was intensely rigid, perfectionistic, or driven. They were churchgoing folk who took life in stride.

A piece of the puzzle was missing. It *had* to be.

Sarah recounted her years in high school and college in vivid detail. Cheerleading. Dance. Church choir. Gymnastics. Perfect grades. Scholarships. Sports awards. Titles. Then, in her third year of college, everything changed.

In that year her grandmother died, and Sarah was raped.

When she reached that point in her story, Sarah's reflections became blurred, and her account became fragmented.

That double-edged trauma became the hinge on which the rest of Sarah's life turned. The loss of her innocence and her confidante were more than she could bear, and, like an anesthetic, the eating disorder became her tool to numb the pain. Gymnastics and college became a thing of the past. The bubbly brunette withdrew from life and went into hiding—for *years*. Then, eighteen years later, she heard me speak in a conference about growing in hard places and made an appointment to see me.

Sarah spent several months in therapy, acknowledging, revisiting, and processing the trauma she had tucked away in secret. Facing the truth about her losses and how they affected her life gradually defused the power of her pain. Each week I saw change. At first tears and, eventually, spontaneous smiles broke through the barrier of Sarah's cold stares. Bit by bit, stone by stone, she dismantled the wall she had built around her heart and risked letting the pain out and others in.

In time, Sarah gained the courage to join a therapy group I

facilitated for women in recovery. One night the group wanted to talk about "God issues" and how they perceived God's involvement in their lives. I passed out paper and markers and asked each member to draw a picture that illustrated her relationship with God.

One woman drew a stick figure of herself—no face, no hair, no clothes—kneeling on one side of a stone wall that towered high above her. Her face was buried in her hands. Bright sunlight shone on the other side of the wall, where Jesus stood with scores of other stick figures. She described herself as someone who was on the outside looking in. "I feel as if God has all kinds of friends down here on earth," she said, "but I'm not one of them."

As we went around the circle, each woman showed the others her picture. When it was Sarah's turn, she held up a likeness of two very large hands holding the handles of an ornate vase. There were many colored markers she could have used, but she chose to do her picture strictly in black. The outline of the vase was carefully drawn and perfectly symmetrical, but down the middle of the vase she had drawn a thick, jagged line depicting a very deep crack. Her description moved me.

"This vase," she said slowly, "can't be fixed. The hands holding it are about to throw it away."

It wasn't a pretty picture, but, even so, Sarah took a step forward that night. For the first time in eighteen years she was truthful with herself and others about how she felt concerning her relationship with God.

I always marvel at God's sovereignty in putting groups together. One of the other members, Terry, immediately stepped in and asked Sarah *how* the vase had become cracked. Terry, herself a rape victim, happened to be nearing the end of her recovery. Within the safety of the group, Sarah was able to uncover the shame-filled events she had hidden for years. I had a front-row seat as I watched God do a deep work in Sarah through those women who offered her acceptance, grace, and truth.

Sarah's bitterness began to change in subtle ways. It didn't happen fast, but, then, long-term change rarely does. As the months passed the eating disorder simply became less and less of an issue. Why? Because the pain driving her compulsion was losing its power. Sarah was learning to face her pain and let it go, so there was less need for an "anesthetic."

One day Sarah walked into my office and said, "I've made a decision. I want to be trained to work on the Rape Crisis Hotline." She didn't want others to suffer in silence or live in denial, as she had for so many years. She wanted to be a refuge for those who were scared and hiding. She wanted God to use her brokenness to help others heal. She wanted others to know that there was hope.

Toward the end of Sarah's recovery, the group again raised "God issues." I had saved the pictures from the previous session and brought them out for review. Each of the women received a clean sheet of paper and colored markers, and when they were finished they showed the others their new drawings.

Sarah's new picture intrigued me. Guessing at its implications, I felt a surge of excitement. Once again she drew a perfectly symmetrical vase with swirly handles on the sides. Once again, the same two large hands firmly gripped it. The deep crack down the middle of the vase was still there too.

But Sarah had added something new. Using a fluorescent yellow marker, she had drawn heavy lines, like beams of light, spilling out of the fissure and flowing to the edge of the paper. Pointing to the crack she said, "*That's* where God shines through."

As the others reflected on her drawing, one woman said,

"Hey, it looks more like a *trophy* than a vase to me."

"Yes!" said another who knew Sarah's story. "You're in God's hands. You're a trophy of His grace." The rest of the women nodded.

Once again I was reminded that it is through our suffering, our trials, and our wounds that God's glory is often revealed. The caption under Sarah's picture could have read "2 Corinthians 4":

> For God, who said, "Let light shine out of darkness," made his light shine in our hearts to give us the light of the knowledge of the glory of God in the face of Christ. But we have this treasure in jars of clay to show that this all-surpassing power is from God and not from us. We are hard pressed on every side, but not crushed; perplexed, but not in despair; persecuted, but not abandoned; struck down, but not destroyed.
>
> Therefore we do not lose heart. Though outwardly we are wasting away, yet inwardly we are being renewed day by day. For our light and momentary troubles are achieving for us an eternal glory that far outweighs them all. So we fix our eyes not on what is seen, but on what is unseen. For what is seen is temporary, but what is unseen is eternal (2 Corinthians 4:6–9, 16–18).

Unadorned clay pots. Vases with cracks. Earthenware jars with chips and dings and flaws. People with troubles, perplexities, weaknesses, traumas, and fears. That's all we are...without God.

But *with* God...oh, we are so much more.

With God, we are people with a treasure inside, a treasure whose value is beyond price, reckoning, or comprehension. We are men and women with God's glory at work in us. His work doesn't entail removing our weaknesses or hardships. No, His work is displayed as He releases His divine power *through* our weaknesses.

When life is hard and God is in us, our broken places can become the windows where His glory shines through.

When life is hard and God is in us, we who are broken pots can become trophies.

When life is hard and God is in us, we can rest assured that somehow, in some way, He will bring His redeeming glory to bear in our lives and in the lives of others.

The longer I work with trauma victims, the more I am convinced that if a heart is open and truthful there is *no* pain so deep or pervasive that God cannot heal it. And, as with Sarah, the broken places of our lives—the fractures, fissures, and jagged edges—can become the very locales where God's glory spills through in a torrent of light, hope, and healing. Out of our own personal darkness, God's penetrating light can touch those who still grope in the shadows.

Just ask one of the regulars on the Rape Crisis Hotline.

Chapter Four

REVIEW THE FACTS

You gain strength, courage and confidence by every experience in which you really stop and look fear in the face. You are able to say to yourself, "I've lived through this... I can take the next thing that comes along." You must do the thing you think you cannot do.

ELEANOR ROOSEVELT

ecently I experienced a rush of anxiety after an innocent mishap. I gave Nathan his nighttime medication and then left the rest of the family at home while I ran a few errands. An hour later I walked in the door toting an armload of groceries. My husband, John, offered to help carry packages in from the garage. Passing me in the hallway, he said, "You don't need to give Nathan his medicine tonight—I already did."

Instantly my brain jumped into 911 mode. *Danger* alarms sounded.

We had a problem. John didn't know that I had already given Nathan his pill, so now Nathan had a double dose of medication in his body. The medicine was something new we were trying for his ADHD (Attention Deficit Hyperactivity Disorder), and I didn't know the drug's toxicity levels or the potential side effects of higher doses. Fear of the unknown revved up my "obsess-o-meter."

One way to reduce worry and anxiety is to get the facts. For me that meant immediately getting on the phone with a friend who is a doctor and a professional educator specializing in that kind of medication. I asked specific questions about how the medicine acted on the brain and what range of dosage was safe for Nathan's body size. From our brief conversation I learned that Nathan could tolerate the double dose and that he would most likely just feel a little groggy for a while. In the words of the expert, "There was no harm done." Those facts brought me peace.

Naomi, a former client, spoke with me one afternoon about the worries that tormented her. As we reviewed her history I learned that a teenage neighbor boy had sexually violated her when she was seven years old. When she came to see me, her oldest son was in the first grade, and Naomi was extremely fearful that what had happened to her would also happen to him.

"Bobby keeps getting invitations to spend the night at his friends' homes," Naomi explained. "I can't let him go. I'm so afraid that something bad might happen to him." Naomi knew that her anxiety was blown out of proportion, but she still couldn't shake it. One of my goals was to help her understand her fears.

"Naomi, the avoidance you're using to cope with these situations is actually driving your anxiety," I said. "This is not the kind of fear you can retreat from in the hope that it will just go away. If you want to beat this fear, you're going to have to face it head-on. You see, the fact is: Avoidance increases anxiety."

Naomi spent the next few months of therapy revisiting and processing her childhood trauma. As she connected her current feelings with the facts of her abuse and grieved the injustice, the pain slowly but surely began to lose its power. One of Naomi's assignments in therapy was to make a list of the facts about her past experience. She then compared it with a list of the facts surrounding Bobby's life. Seeing the specific differences in black and white brought her a measure of relief.

But there was more work to do. Naomi decided to give her son some important information. She bought a children's book about personal safety and taught Bobby how to pay attention to the "uh-oh" in his tummy. He learned that it was very important to "Say no!" and to "Go and tell" an adult if he felt at risk. She rehearsed potential scenarios with Bobby and showed him how to respond to someone who was acting in a sexually inappropriate way. Giving Bobby the facts reduced Naomi's concerns about his vulnerability and increased her confidence in his ability to protect himself.

Gathering facts about Bobby's friends and their parents was also helpful. Naomi felt more comfortable with some individuals than with others. She reached a great milestone when she and her husband gave Bobby permission to spend the night with his best friend after a ball game. It didn't happen without some anxiety, but it happened!

To keep herself from worrying, Naomi used a diversion tactic that evening: She and her husband went to see an action-packed movie. During our next counseling session she happily reported that she had slept well through the night. As for Bobby, when he came home in the morning he was beaming.

YEARS AGO I SAW a clever acrostic for the word fear: False Evidence Appearing Real. When we are fearful, we tend to jump to conclusions based on partial truth instead of on complete and accurate evidence. When something goes wrong and we don't have the facts, we can misinterpret the meaning of an event and immediately forecast the worst-case scenario.

I've heard it said that the more intelligent and creative you are, the more likely you are to worry. Why? Because when people are worried about something, their imaginations paint mental pictures of what they dread most. Those with sharp minds see all the angles of a given predicament, and their creativity enables them to vividly envision every possible miserable outcome.

Are worries stealing your joy? Are anxieties eating away at your peace of mind? If so, may I make a suggestion? Please—get the facts. If you're fretting about the possibility of a health problem, don't brood over it. Call a doctor or see a specialist who can review the facts with you. Focus your attention on *what is*, not on *what if*. Investigate. Ask questions. Research. Pool information. A mind that feeds on the facts is less likely to fall prey to a frenzied imagination that casts illusions as reality. The fear of the unknown can paralyze you, but reviewing the facts can set you free and give you peace.

Chapter Five

REMAIN IN
THE PRESENT

*Anxiety is not only a pain which we must ask God to assuage
but also a weakness we must ask Him to pardon—
for He's told us to take no care for the morrow.*

C. S. LEWIS

*M*any of our worries come from a tendency to overestimate
the probability of a harmful event and to exaggerate its
potential negative impact. Peering into the future, our imaginations
run wild, leading us to conclude that things are going to turn out
badly and with unbearable results.

One of the best ways to stop this needless waste of mental and
emotional energy is to live in the moment—not tomorrow, not next
week, not next month, but today, right now.

Let me guess how you might be responding at this moment:
Easier said than done, Pam.

You're right. The doing isn't always easy. Our minds like to wander from the present, particularly when our thought processes aren't
focused on something stimulating.

Recently I found myself struggling to keep my thoughts in the
moment. John and I have a friend who comes to our home every
once in a while to give us a massage. There I was, on the massage

table, enjoying the warmth of a crackling fire, the melodies of sooth-ing classical music, and the touch of gifted hands, when I suddenly felt a knot in my stomach. I soon realized that my mind was chew-ing on some problems that needed to be solved before our family traveled out of the country the following week.

While I rehearsed the logistics of the trip, the what ifs led me down rabbit trails into anxiety. I imagined us getting bumped from a flight and spending the night in an airport with our three kids. That's not my idea of fun!

Stop it, I told myself. *You can deal with the details of the trip later. Now is not the time.* To bring myself back to the moment, I took several deep cleansing breaths, refocused on the crackling fire, the music, and the sensations my body was feeling from the massage. A few minutes later, when my stomach knotted up once more, I realized that I was off in the future again.

I had to bring myself back to focusing on the here and now three times before my mind finally let go of the impending trip! As long as I stayed in the moment, my body was peaceful and worry-free. When I was in the future, my stomach told the story.

By the way, our bodies never lie. They send clear cues to us about what is going on in our minds. We do ourselves a favor when we lis-ten to what our bodies are saying.

Focusing our attention on the moment requires mental disci-pline, but the contentment it brings is worth it. I can hear you saying, "Now, wait a minute. Isn't it a bit ridiculous to expect myself not to think about the future? How else can I plan for what lies ahead?"

I'm not saying that we should never think about the future. That's silly. A well-ordered life requires us to plan. Thinking ahead makes sense when it's related to necessary planning, but it can become a problem when most of our thoughts have little connection with the here and now. What I am saying is that we need to try to live in the present *more* than we live in the future. When our minds perpetually spin forward into the future, we generate anxiety and miss the joy of the immediate.

You see, our thoughts powerfully influence our feelings. In a matter of seconds they can destroy our peaceful states of mind and create panicked anxiety—even though nothing in our present situations has changed at all.

A few nights ago, after my husband and I tucked our two youngest children into bed, I hopped into bed myself, nestled under the covers, and opened a good book. There I was, snuggled beneath my warm electric blanket and lost in a story, when a thought occurred to me: *It's ten-thirty, and Jessie isn't home yet.* Our teenage daughter had a ten-thirty curfew, but she hadn't yet walked through the front door. I brushed it off, figuring that the traffic was bad.

I went back to my book. Ten minutes later, Jessie still wasn't home. This time I didn't brush it off as well. My mind wandered: *It's not like her not to be home on time. I wonder what's going on. I hope she's okay. Why didn't she call to tell me she'd be late?*

Countering the anxious thoughts, I told myself that there was probably a good reason why she was late. But my worry intensified when my creative imagination conjured up a troublesome scene: her friend's car broken down and the kids stuck on the side of the road with no one to help. I overestimated the likelihood that she was in trouble and the probability that the results were going to be harmful.

By the time Jessie arrived home thirty minutes later, my mind was anything but calm and serene. She wasn't home on time, and I didn't like it. Coming back to the present allowed me to maintain my cool. I told myself, *She's home. She's safe. Now listen to her.* Had I persisted in my anxious imaginations, my agitation would have reached a boiling point and erupted all over her. Fortunately I was able to contain myself and not blow a fuse before I heard her explanation. (There have been other times when I flunked the test of self-control and my pot did boil over, making matters worse, not better.) On this particular night I did better. And my fears, as you might expect, were unfounded.

All of the pent-up emotion in my body was simply a by-product of my unchecked, future-oriented thoughts. Once I reviewed the facts and directed my attention back to the present, peace returned to me. If I had simply kept my mental energies in the here and now, enjoyed my warm blanket and book, and reminded myself of my daughter's resourcefulness and common sense, I would have saved myself a lot of unnecessary grief.

When we forecast gloom and doom into our futures or go back into the past and rake up all the troubles we've had, we end up reeling and staggering through life. Stability and peace of mind come by living in the moment.

Where are your thoughts focused? Are you engaged in what you're currently doing? How foolish and counterproductive is it to allow our imaginations to run wild into a future that not only doesn't exist but may never exist. Most of our worries are imaginary. Most of the dangers we fear have no life outside our worries and speculations.

Are there real dangers? Real hazards? Real crises? Certainly. And God will give us the grace to face each and every one of them as they cross our paths. But in the meantime, let's embrace each new day of life—with all its joys, opportunities, and challenges—and, by His grace, live it to the full.

Reclaim Your Life

FOOD FOR THOUGHT

Peace is not arbitrary. It must be based upon definite facts. God has all the facts on His side; the world does not. Therefore God, and not the world, can give peace.

BILLY GRAHAM

PRAYER FOR TODAY

Lord, I'm struggling with a multitude of worries. Some of it comes from things in my past that I cannot change. And my heart and mind race to the future and what could or might happen. Father, please ground me in the present. Help me to acknowledge the facts of my current circumstances and to realize that I can't change the past or the future. Please focus my thoughts on You and on today. And please bring peace to my heart. In Your name, amen.

STEPS TO TAKE THIS MONTH

- List the facts of your situation. What are anxiety and emotion telling you that simply isn't true?

- Embrace your current situation. Be brutally honest about your pain and look truth in the face.

- Pay attention to what your body is telling you. Are you dwelling too much on what *could* happen or what *did* happen? Ask the Lord to help you stay in the present.

CONNECT WITH GOD

~

*And then there is time in which to be, simply to be,
that time in which God quietly tells us who we are and who He
wants us to be. It is then that God can take our emptiness and
fill it up with what He wants, and drain away the business with
which we inevitably get involved in the dailiness of human living.*

MADELEINE L'ENGLE

Chapter Six

RELINQUISH
YOUR AGENDA

A number of years ago I was invited to speak at a major women's conference. At the time I wondered why God even had me there, because He and I were in the middle of an intense power struggle.

Bottom line: I was pregnant for the fourth time, and I didn't want to be pregnant.

John and I were "finished having children," and it seemed to me that the Lord ought to have been well aware of that fact. We already had a daughter, Jessie, and a son, Benjamin. Our first baby was safe in heaven, and, with one child of each flavor, we were balanced—content, comfortable. It was "us four and no more," and we loved it that way. We loved our ministry. Life was working out very nicely.

Then, out of the blue, I turned up pregnant.

How could it be? Well, I knew how it could be, but it shouldn't have been! We had taken all the necessary precautions. Somehow this baby was conceived in spite of the foolproof birth-control method we had used for seventeen years.

I guess we didn't have as much control as I thought. Life has a knack for teaching us that control is really an illusion.

At the time, my emotions resembled a tossed salad—a wedge of guilt here, a slice or two of anger there, with some self-pity sprinkled over the top for spice.

I felt guilt because I had friends who wanted so very much to get pregnant and couldn't, and here I was upset that the little test stick had turned blue.

I felt anger because my agenda had been interrupted and rearranged.

I felt self-pity because I was sick all day, every day, through most of the pregnancy.

One morning during the conference, I had some time off the platform, so I ordered breakfast in my room, read in the Gospel of John, and journaled my thoughts and feelings. I can assure you, God got an earful.

But then, after I had vented, it was His turn.

Through the years the Lord has at times made some things very clear to me, and this was one of those times. As I was reading John 15, I came across a familiar passage that jolted me like a double dose of smelling salts. Jesus was speaking: "I am the true vine, and my Father is the gardener. He cuts off every branch in me that bears no fruit, while every branch that does bear fruit he prunes so that it will be even more fruitful" (John 15:1-2).

As I read those verses I sensed God saying to me, *Pam, you're not being set back—you're being cut back.*

In that instant a picture of the three rose bushes in our front yard came to my mind. Each summer the trees produce huge, yellow, long-stemmed roses that fill our home with a glorious fragrance. Arranged in a vase on a table, the blooms seem to glow with a golden light of their own.

But in the fall, John cuts them back. Way back. After his pruning shears do the job, I look at those stumps and think, *My goodness, the man is ruthless. Those poor things look decapitated!*

Every fall I wonder if they'll ever grow back. But sure enough, every spring they do.

Pam, you're not being set back—you're being cut back.

In the quiet of that hotel room I knew that God was up to something in my life and that my pregnancy had in no way caught Him by surprise. For some incomprehensible reason, this was part of His plan to produce more beauty and fragrance in my life.

Ever so reluctantly I waved my little white flag. *Okay, Lord,* I said. *I surrender to You.*

That was no small first step! I wish I could say that it had been easier for me. How do you and I let go of the disappointments and losses that we've suffered? We relinquish control. We surrender.

But not to "fate." Not to our emotions. Not to bitterness. No, we deliberately yield the control of our lives to God.

Oh, yes, it all sounds nice enough—and spiritual to boot. But, friend, surrender isn't always such a tidy bundle. Often it's a messy package of painful feelings like anger, rage, and deep sadness, which eventually give way to release and peace. As we surrender, we often feel frustrated and angry at God, at other people, at ourselves, and at life.

Oftentimes our saying, *Yes, Lord,* simply opens the door to the grieving process. We suddenly find ourselves at the very core of our pain and sadness: the heavy emotional burden that has to be released before we can feel right again. By allowing the grief to enter through the front door of surrender, healing can slip in, quiet and unannounced, through the back door.

The tendency is strong to say,
"...God won't be so stern as to

expect me to give up that!" but he will;
"He won't expect me to walk in the light so
that I have nothing to hide" but he will;
"He won't expect me to draw on his
grace for everything" but he will.

OSWALD CHAMBERS

WILLPOWER ISN'T the key. Letting go is.

For many years I've heard men and women from all walks of life say things like:

"I've invested too many years of my life trying to make people be what they don't want to be or do what they don't want to do. I've driven them—and myself—crazy in the process."

"I spent my childhood trying to make an angry father who didn't love himself be a normal person who loved me."

I've spent years trying to make emotionally unavailable people be emotionally present for me."

"I've poured my life into trying to make unhappy family members happy, even though they don't seem interested in making the slightest effort."

"I've given the last twenty-five years of my life to trying to make my alcoholic husband stop drinking."

What they are all saying is something like this: "I've spent much of my life desperately and vainly trying to do the impossible and feeling like a dismal failure when I can't." It's like planting carrot seeds and trying passionately, creatively, and desperately to make those little plants grow prize tomatoes—and feeling defeated when it doesn't work.

By relinquishing control and surrendering to God, we gain the presence of mind to stop wasting time and energy trying to change and control things that we can't change or control. Surrender gives us permission to stop trying to do the impossible and to focus on what is possible.

I wish I could say that surrender, letting go, is a one-time event. As I mentioned in the previous chapter, it's not. Yielding to the Lord is a continual, daily, sometimes hourly process. When God and I were locked in a wrestling match in that hotel room, it was only round one. Unbeknownst to me, down the road there were many more rounds to go.

Less than three months later our baby arrived, six weeks early and with a few surprises of his own. On the day Nathan was born, something was wrong—terribly wrong. He was blue, not breathing well, and his little cry sounded muted. Instead of placing him in my waiting arms, the technicians scurried around trying to help him breathe. John held my hands, and we prayed for Nathan, asking God to help him and to guide the doctors' efforts.

I kept asking the nurses if Nathan was all right, but all I could get out of them was "He's in good hands" and "They're helping clear his passageways." When I asked if I could nurse him, they said they didn't know. An hour later, impatient with vague answers and frustrated about being separated from my son, I asked the delivery nurse to wheel me into the care unit where they were working with Nathan. The pediatrician on call came over to talk with us. I didn't know this woman, and I didn't want to believe a word she was saying.

"Mrs. Vredevelt, your son is not oxygenating well, so we're trying to help him with oxygen and IVs."

"Is this life-threatening?" I asked.

"It could be," she replied. "It's also my observation that he has Down's syndrome. I've called a cardiologist to examine him because I think his heart isn't functioning properly."

At that point I wasn't tracking well and blurted out, "What does this mean?"

"It means he will be mentally retarded, Mrs. Vredevelt. There is also a higher incidence of leukemia for those with Down's syndrome. There's a catheter in his heart, and the technicians are still working to stabilize him."

I spent that night alone in my room, listening to happy families around me celebrating their babies. My own doctor was in Russia. My pediatrician was on vacation. My parents were in California. John and the kids were home in bed, and a tiny boy named Nathan Vredevelt was in a sterile room under impersonal fluorescent lights, fighting for his life.

And me? I began to wonder just how much God really loved me. As hot tears rolled down my cheeks, I whispered into the night, *God, what is this? A bad joke? Well, I'm not laughing!*

The next morning the cardiologist ran a battery of tests on Nathan. Based on the results, he said, the center section of Nathan's heart was not formed, and he would likely need open-heart surgery at the age of four months. During surgery the doctor would construct the center portions of Nathan's heart so he could oxygenate better and grow more normally.

When the cardiologist left the room, wild and unchecked ruminations entered my mind. What if Nathan's heart fails and he doesn't make it to four months? What if the surgery doesn't work?

What if he gets sick and his body isn't strong enough to fight infection? How do we raise a child with Down's syndrome? What if Jessie and Ben can't adjust to having a handicapped brother? What if...? What if...?

Round two of the wrestling match had begun.

Have you ever wrestled with God? Jacob did. Remember him? He lied to his blind, aged father and eventually stole his brother's inheritance rights—the most precious thing a man could possess. The name *Jacob* means "crafty deceiver," and Jacob tried hard to live up to his name.

Ah, but there came a night when this son of Isaac slipped through the ropes in the darkness and climbed into the ring with the angel of the Lord:

> Jacob was left alone, and a man wrestled with him till daybreak. When the man saw that he could not overpower him, he touched the socket of Jacob's hip so that his hip was wrenched as he wrestled with the man. Then the man said, "Let me go, for it is daybreak."
>
> But Jacob replied, "I will not let you go unless you bless me."
>
> The man asked him, "What is your name?"
>
> "Jacob," he answered.
>
> Then the man said, "Your name will no longer be Jacob, but Israel, because you have struggled with God and with men and have overcome."
>
> Jacob said, "Please tell me your name."
>
> But he replied, "Why do you ask my name?" Then he blessed him there.
>
> So Jacob called the place Peniel, saying, "It is because I saw God face to face, and yet my life was spared."

The sun rose above him as he passed Peniel, and he was limping because of his hip. (Genesis 32:24-31)

The text says that God allowed Jacob to prevail, but before He let His man up off the mat, He dislocated Jacob's hip. Let me assure you, friend, a dislocated hip isn't a hangnail or a bad hair day. It's an extremely painful condition. And through all the years that followed, it was a constant reminder to Jacob that he was not to depend on his own strength. He was to rely entirely on God.

God loves us so much that He will wrestle with us. He's not going to give us everything we want all the time. That night when Jacob was alone in the dark, he wrestled with God—and God blessed his life. In spite of Jacob's seedy track record, in spite of his scheming, manipulative, and deceitful ways, God chose to open heaven's great storehouses and pour His favor out upon him. (Why does that encourage me so much?) From that point on, Jacob knew that his well-being was dependent on God's help, God's guidance, and God's blessing, not on his own devices. He gave up control.

It's a lesson about letting God be God—a lesson that I'll be working on every day until the Lord says it's time for me to exit this world and follow Him home.

While we were in the hospital, the people in our church prayed for Nathan at a Wednesday evening service. That very evening his vital signs took a turn for the better. His oxygenation improved, and by morning the doctor was able to remove the IV from Nathan's heart. Four days later, during the Sunday morning services, the congregation prayed for Nathan again. This time they prayed specifically for the healing of his heart.

Mom flew into town to help us, and on the following Tuesday she and I took Nathan to the hospital for more tests. The cardiologist wanted to examine all the cross sections of Nathan's heart on the ultrasound screen in order to determine how much of the heart muscle needed to be constructed.

We watched the screens intently as he focused on various chambers of the heart. When he got a clear shot of the center section, he started to shake his head and chuckle. Then, in his clipped British accent, he announced happily, "By golly, the center of his heart is absolutely normal!"

I started to cry, my mom started to cry, and the doctor just kept shaking his head in amazement, muttering, "Very good, oh, very good."

Then he pointed to a small hole between the upper and lower chambers of the heart, showing us on the screen where the blood was spilling through. After taking some measurements, he consulted with us in his office.

"Mrs. Vredevelt," he said, "Nathan has two small holes in his heart. I want to watch them for the next six months and see if they will close on their own. If they do, surgery won't be necessary. If they don't, we'll need to patch them when he's a little older."

I cried, my mom cried, and the doctor beamed broadly, telling us how much he enjoyed giving good news. The presence of two small holes was much better news than any of us had expected. During the following six months a host of friends around the country prayed for Nathan, and at his next appointment the cardiologist told us that the holes had closed. We no longer had to be concerned about surgery.

I left the hospital that day with a renewed awareness: God is still in the business of healing. That truth applies to baby boys with holes in their hearts and to grown-up women with holes in their faith.

Either way, when we put everything in His hands, His is the touch that heals.

Chapter Seven

RUN TO GOD

There is rarely a complete silence in our soul.
God is whispering to us well nigh incessantly.
Whenever the sounds of the world die out in the soul, or sink low,
then we hear these whisperings of God. He is always whispering
to us, only we do not always hear because of the noise, hurry,
and distraction which life causes as it rushes on.

FREDERICK WILLIAM FABER

*I*n our times of letting go, God is the one we need to run to because He knows us better than we know ourselves.

Run to God. It sounds so basic. But when we're distressed, our natural tendency is often to retreat from everyone, including God. We run in all kinds of directions by keeping ourselves excessively busy. We turn to activities, food, alcohol, novels, shopping, entertainment, and other people to mask our pain. Rollo May said it well: "It is an old and ironic habit of human beings to run faster when we have lost our way."

God is the Specialist who can give us insight into our needs.

He's the Guide who can offer direction when we're disoriented.

He's the Caretaker of our souls who can give us strength and courage when we're afraid to let go.

Scripture provides a sturdy signpost when we find ourselves on a dangerous road:

Trust in the LORD with all your heart
> and lean not on your own understanding;
in all your ways acknowledge him,
> and he will make your paths straight. (Proverbs 3:5–6)

One of the best coping skills that I know of for dealing with the painful realities of life is to tune your mind-set to watch for God's activities. You'll find what you're looking for.

Look around you right now. Find five things that are the color green or have green in them. With your mind-set tuned to look for green, the color green will start to jump out at you. Your eye will be drawn to a green shirt, a green book, leaves on flowers, a green notebook or pen.

Have you ever noticed that after you've bought a new car, you begin to notice every other car like yours on the road? People find what they are looking for. If you're looking for conspiracies, you'll find them. If you're looking for God's perfect plan, you'll find it too.

When Nathan was diagnosed with Down's syndrome, John and I were abruptly faced with the difficult assignment of letting go of many things that we held near and dear to our hearts. We had to let go of our agenda for our lives, of our dreams for a healthy baby, of my professional position because much more of my energy was needed at home, of once-cherished areas of church involvement, of some of our free time, of my creative writing for five years, and of a few relationships due to lack of time and cultivation. It was a dark season of grief for all of us.

But perspective arrived in an unexpected package one afternoon shortly after we brought Nathan home from the hospital. I received a phone call from a friend. Knowing that I had my hands full trying to adjust to so many changes, Kay said, "I'm coming over to clean your house. What's a good day?"

Kay showed up on my doorstep a couple of days later with our friend, Delight. What a sight greeted me when I opened the front door! Those two looked like they had just stepped off the set of a science fiction movie. They wore buckets on their heads, gas masks on their faces, combat boots, striped socks, and aprons over outfits that would have been rejected by the homeless.

They had come to make me laugh. And it worked!

Kay and Delight's visit was far more significant to me than the laughter—or the clean floors and dusted furniture they left behind. Kay is the mother of two, Kurt and Kara. We had known the family for many years because their son was in our youth group years ago when John and I worked with teenagers. Kara, their youngest, had been born with cerebral palsy and over the years had undergone extensive surgical procedures. For twelve years Kay had walked the path I was just beginning to walk.

When I saw her standing there in that crazy getup on my porch, smiling from ear to ear, I remembered the many times when I had seen her in the past and thought, *She has such burdens. How can she be so happy?*

I plopped myself in our big stuffed chair in the living room to nurse Nathan and said, "Kay, I'm struggling with something. I don't know how to view Nathan's handicap from God's perspective. How do you see it?"

Wise lady that she is, Kay didn't give me any platitudes or pat answers. Instead, she pointed me to Scripture. One of the passages that had been meaningful to her family since Kara's birth, she told me, was John 9. I had my copy of *The Message* at hand. Eager for some answers, I immediately picked it up and began to read:

Walking down the street, Jesus saw a man blind from birth. His disciples asked, "Rabbi, who sinned: this man or his parents, causing him to be born blind?"

Jesus said, "You're asking the wrong question. You're looking for someone to blame. There is no such cause-effect here. Look instead for what God can do."

(John 9:1-3, *The Message*)

Those verses gave me a fresh perspective that brisk fall afternoon. They challenged me to look for God in the midst of my daily grind. I resolved to quit trying to figure it all out and to believe that God would be working in our family as we made the adjustments needed to welcome Nathan.

Look instead for what God can do. I pondered those words for a long time as I held Nathan that day. I wondered how the blind man felt before Jesus came into his life. My hunch is that he assumed he would always be shrouded in darkness. Little did he know that he was headed for historical significance. Little did he know that one day he would stand boldly before the religious leaders of Jerusalem and testify to God's healing power in his life.

Who can give you and me the ability to believe that we have a future?

God.

Who can give you and me the faith to believe that our children are in God's hands—no matter what?

God.

Who can give us the faith to believe that God will have His way in our children's lives when circumstances seem to be pointing another direction?

God.

God challenges you and me to let go of our efforts to make sense out of unexpected enigmas and to have eyes of faith for ourselves, our children, our marriages, our jobs, and our ministries. He says, "I know the plans I have for you.... They are plans for good and not for evil, to give you a future and a hope.... When you pray, I will listen. You will find me when you seek me, if you look for me in earnest" (Jeremiah 29:11–13, TLB).

God, with a full awareness of our weaknesses, wounds, handicaps, and disappointments, challenges us to run to Him, to place our trust in Him—even when our hearts are breaking, even when our logic screams that He doesn't care or that He has made a terrible mistake.

In the end, He will use us in His own special way. He will orchestrate our unique, divine assignments. And nothing can stop Him from achieving His purposes.

In the midst of the pain and confusion that often accompany letting go, we need to run to God and say, *God, I need Your help. Give me Your perspective. Let my eyes see as You see. Let my heart hear Your heart. Grant me insight into what You are doing in my life right now. Show me what I need to do to cooperate with You in my healing.*

And then, dear friend, pay very close attention to the people who cross your path and the situations that present themselves. Be mindful of the insights that bubble to the surface and the whisperings of the Holy Spirit, because God will be faithful to answer those kinds of prayers.

Chapter Eight

REGISTER
YOUR CONCERNS

Don't fret or worry. Instead of worrying, pray.
Let petitions and praises shape your worries into prayers,
letting God know your concerns.
Before you know it, a sense of God's wholeness,
everything coming together for good,
will come and settle you down.

PHILIPPIANS 4:6-7, THE MESSAGE

My secretary stood in the doorway of my office, her face registering her alarm. "Pam, you have an emergency phone call," she said. "Nathan left the school yard. They've searched for the last half hour and can't find him, so they're calling the police."

That news would send icy shivers through any mother, but my fear escalated in light of my son's Down's syndrome. Nathan lacks the safety net of common sense and maturity, and when he wanders outside of adult supervision, his risk of encountering danger increases exponentially.

Adrenaline coursing through my veins, I rushed to the phone that my secretary held for me. "Hello, this is Pam," I said, trying to maintain my cool. "I'm on my way."

It's astounding what anxiety does to the body. By the time I reached my car my stomach was in knots, and a lump the size of a ping-pong ball seemed wedged against my larynx. I began playing therapist with myself.

Okay, Pam. Calm down. God knows right where Nathan is. There are a lot of people looking for him. Keep your cool. Don't jump to conclusions. You won't be any help to anybody if you start short-circuiting. Just relax. You'll be at the school in five minutes.

That was the plan.

But you know how plans go.

When I started the car, a buzzer signaled that my gas tank was empty. I had intended to get gas on the way to work that morning, but, running late, I figured I could make it to the office and fill the tank after work.

Now, what do you think a professional therapist would do in a situation like that? Would she respond with logic and say, "Hmm. It looks like I need gas"? Would she maintain complete composure, casually shrug, and say, "Oh well, what's another kink in the day"? Or would she flail her hands, scream, "Oh no!" at the gas gauge, and then burst into tears?

You guessed it! Obviously my car wasn't the only thing running on fumes at the moment. After my little fit, I pulled myself together long enough to pray, *God, please get me to the gas station that's on the way to the school.*

He did. But I should have prayed for the people who worked at the station, because they were slower than slugs on a Portland sidewalk. For several l-o-o-o-n-g minutes my car was the only one at the pumps, but no one responded. If the Lord was testing my patience, I flunked. After waiting and waiting, I finally went into the station and said, "Could someone please help me? I'm in a hurry. My little boy is lost, and I need to go find him."

The guy dawdling behind the counter acted as if he didn't have a care in the world. He cocked his head to the side, squinted his eyes, and gave me the look. You know, the one that says, "Yeah, sure, lady." He s-l-o-o-o-w-l-y made his way to the pumps.

Twelve and a half minutes later I rolled out of the station with enough repressed negative energy in my body to trigger another eruption on Mount St. Helens.

Panic-driven thoughts ricocheted in my brain. *What if we can't find Nathan? What if he wanders onto a busy street? What if a felon gets hold of him?* Pictures on milk cartons flashed before my eyes. A vivid imagination is a blessing for creative writing, but it's a curse in that kind of situation.

I finally arrived at the school. Racing up to the front doors, I passed a woman walking toward the parking lot. I must have had *panicked mother* written all over my face, because she looked at me and asked, "Are you Nathan's mom?"

"Yes," I responded anxiously, hoping she had some good news for me.

"They found Nathan."

"Oh, thank God," I said.

"He's with the principal," she added.

Sure enough, there in the principal's office sat my guilty little escapee. I couldn't remember an occasion when Nathan hadn't smiled and jumped up to give me a welcoming hug after we'd been apart for a few hours. But this time he had a very somber look on his face, and he didn't move. His head hung low, and he looked at me through guilty eyes, knowing he had made a big boo-boo.

I hugged him. "Nathan," I said gently, "I was very worried about you. And the principal and your teachers were scared too. Leaving the schoolyard was not a good idea."

The principal gave me the full story. Somehow Nathan had sneaked around to the back of the school, pushed the gate open, and wandered over to the retirement home next door. He went to the third floor of the complex (Nathan loves elevators and is proficient at working them), roamed the halls, and then went back down to the ground level and out the back door. I guess he'd seen enough of the old folks and decided it was time for something a bit more exciting.

Driven by his unquenchable thirst for adventure, he bolted over to the next building on the block, which happened to be a hospital. There a kind elderly man noticed that Nathan was handicapped and all alone in the hospital lobby. Figuring that he was lost, the man took him by the hand and began hunting. A few minutes later, one of the school helpers in the search party rounded the corner.

Nathan spent the rest of the afternoon in the principal's office with the school counselor. She drew pictures of the event to help him understand which choices were acceptable and which were not. I am so thankful for such sources of support as we try to help Nathan grow up to be safe and wise. Still, I think I pumped more adrenaline during that episode than I had in the entire previous month.

And, boy, oh boy, did my body feel it the next day! When the alarm went off at 5:30 a.m. I felt as if I'd been hit by a Mack truck. The impact wasn't just physical. My mind was troubled, and worry was getting the best of me. My anxiety about the events of the previous day was matched by my apprehension of what was to come.

Do you ever experience that? Ever have a day so full of panic that even after a situation is resolved the residue of fear taints your outlook? At times like that we need to take some time alone to register our concerns with God. He invites us to do so. The apostle Peter wrote: "Cast all your anxiety on him because he cares for you" (1 Peter 5:7). In the original language this phrase means that we are "to aggressively roll over" all of our worries onto God.

Let's think for a moment about how we are created. We are made up of body, soul, and spirit. Through the body's senses we relate to the world around us. The soul is the thinking and feeling part of us: the mind, will, emotions, conscience, and consciousness. The soul allows us to laugh, cry, reason, and make choices. Then there is the spirit, which enables us to relate to God.

I have noticed that human beings tend to use only two-thirds of this package. Even if we try to use the capacities of our bodies and souls to the fullest, we may neglect our spirits. Yet God longs to have a personal relationship with us and to be intimately involved in the things that matter most to us. One of the reasons He invites us to cast our anxieties on Him is that He is far more capable of bearing those burdens than we are. He never intended for us to carry the stresses, strains, and harsh realities of this world on our own shoulders. He wants us to roll them onto Him and to ask Him for what we need.

One of the ways that we can register our concerns with God is by writing them in a prayer journal. Some call it a "worry registry." This is a powerful tool for reducing anxiety, and a number of my clients have benefited from this discipline for years. They buy a new blank book at the beginning of each year and, on a regular basis, record their worries in letters to God.

This kind of journaling serves several purposes. Registering our concerns and needs with God in detail is a very constructive way to defuse the pent-up tension surrounding our worries. Even more importantly, it opens the door for Him to intervene in our lives. We get far better results with His power at work than we do if we depend only on our own limited human resources. Watching concrete, specific answers to prayer unfold over time is a faith-building, life-changing experience. The more people see God answer their prayers, the more they tend to register their concerns.

The morning following Nathan's escape, I made myself a cup of coffee, found a comfortable seat in the living room, jotted down some of my worries, and offered a simple prayer. It was nothing complicated, just a soul's cry for help:

Lord, You know how troubled I am about Nathan. I need You to speak to me today. Please give me Your perspective, and help me hear what You want to say to me this morning.

As I read from my Bible, I wrote down some verses that spoke to me about what had taken center stage in my mind:

I will make springs in the desert, so that my chosen people can be refreshed. (Isaiah 43:20, NLT)

I will give you abundant water to quench your thirst and to moisten your parched fields. And I will pour out my Spirit and my blessings on your children. They will thrive like watered grass, like willows on a riverbank. (44:3–4, NLT)

And I will give you treasures hidden in the darkness—secret riches. I will do this so you may know that I am the LORD...the one who calls you by name. (45:3, NLT)

By {God's} mighty power at work within us, he is able to accomplish infinitely more than we would ever dare to ask or hope. (Ephesians 3:20, NLT)

The sequence and content of the verses rang with meaning. I recorded in my journal what the Lord seemed to be saying to me:

Pam, when life escorts you into a hot, dry, barren desert, look to Me. I always have what you need. I will refresh you. You can never tap the limit of My abundant supply. I have enough for you and your children. I will pour out My Spirit and bless your children today. They will thrive. And in the middle of the hardships and the dark times you endure, I will give you treasures—treasures that can be found only in the dark—that prove that I love you and that I am intimately aware of everything going on in your life. I understand your weaknesses and vulnerabilities. Don't be fooled by your feelings. My Spirit lives in you, and He is able to accomplish more than you have ever imagined. So rest. Trust. Let My words empower you. They are spirit and they are your very life.

I closed my journal that morning with a much healthier outlook on the day. My body still felt bulldozed, but my mind was more settled. Even though nothing had really changed on the outside, I was different on the inside. Order and focus had emerged out of a chaotic mishmash of worry and anxiety. Registering my concerns with God had brought me relief.

Are fears wearing you out? Are you carrying heavy weights of worry that you need to unload? Have you considered placing those burdens in the hands of God? He would like nothing more than to intervene on your behalf. Rest assured that God will hear and He will answer. I haven't met a person yet who has regretted turning to God for help.

Peace comes when we lift our cares to Him—and let them go.

Chapter Nine

RELAX
AND RECEIVE

In time we must release our grip on everything we hold dear.

DR. JAMES DOBSON

*T*ry a little exercise with me. Clench your fist into a ball. Squeeze as hard as you can, and count to ten. Study your hand as you do so.

Ready? Go. S-q-u-e-e-e-z-e.

Okay, now relax.

Let go.

How did your fist feel, gripping so tightly? What did it look like? Can you describe the sensations you felt? How did it feel to release your grip and open your hand after you counted to ten?

When your hand was clenched it was uncomfortable, wasn't it? Tense. Bloodless. Unable to move freely. Not only that, but it wasn't able to do what it was *designed* to do. Your hand was closed, unable to receive. But when you let go and opened your hand, you could feel the blood returning to your fingers, couldn't you? Your hand became warm again. It relaxed, the discomfort left, and you felt relief. Your fingers moved naturally, and your hand was in a much better position to receive.

There are similarities between our physical bodies and our

psyches. When we go through life grasping, clinging, clutching, and desperately trying to hang on to things that should naturally be released, we ache. We get tied up in knots. We become emotionally constricted and locked up in pain. We lose freedom of movement in our lives and feel paralyzed.

Sometimes we hang on tight to our worries in a superstitious sort of way. We think that somehow—illogical as the thought might be—we will be able to *prevent* a negative outcome by worrying. It's as if worry had some sort of mysterious merit. *If I don't stress about this, something really bad will happen!* I see this in people I counsel, and as irrational as I know this line of reasoning to be, I see it in my own life.

For several years, our family traveled to Mexico during spring break to help a few church congregations. John and I offered leadership training, counseling, and teaching, while our children shared skits, music, and mimes with the Hispanic children. These annual mission trips were usually wonderful weeks of work and fun, but one year held some surprises that raised my anxiety quotient to a very uncomfortable level.

Twice while we were traveling in the twelve-passenger van, we barely escaped a head-on collision. The first time we were barreling sixty-five miles an hour down a long, steep hill when a huge bus attempted to pass a slow string of cars on the upgrade. The bus entered our lane traveling sixty miles an hour. There were no shoulders on the road, just jagged cliffs on both sides, so we couldn't pull over. John slammed on the brakes, and the bus came within inches of us before passing the other cars and switching lanes. A big delivery truck did the same thing a few days later, and again we narrowly escaped with our lives.

My worry factor ratcheted up another notch one evening when

Nathan decided to play hide-and-seek without telling anyone. Just before dark our whole family and everyone else who was sitting poolside at the hotel ended up searching the grounds for "the little blond-haired boy with Down's syndrome." I was worried that Nathan had left the hotel commons and was wandering the streets. *Safe* is not a word I would use to describe the surrounding area for an eight-year-old child on the loose. The hotel manager told us that the police probably wouldn't be any help and to "keep looking."

In the middle of our frantic search our older son, Benjamin, ran up to our living quarters to get a bird's-eye view from the balcony. He yelled Nathan's name, and, much to his surprise, Nathan answered. When Ben turned in the direction of his voice, he saw Nathan on the balcony next to ours, hiding under the patio table. He smiled and waved, as if to say, "Tag—you're it!" While we were all very relieved to find him safe and sound, I pumped so much adrenaline in those thirty minutes that three hours later I still felt weak in the knees.

I had accepted an invitation to speak at a women's conference at Mt. Hermon, California, and was scheduled to catch a plane out of Mexico a couple of days ahead of the rest of the family. Wanting to make the most of my last morning on the Baja, I set my alarm early so I could take a long walk on the beach at sunrise. As I strolled the sandy shoreline, I prayed and reflected on the week. The night before had been one of the highlights of the trip. John and I had spoken to a very enthusiastic crowd and then had the joy of praying with many people at the close of the meeting.

One of the women stood out in my mind. Her name was Lucinda. When she approached us asking for prayer, she was obviously in deep emotional turmoil. Her eyes were red and swollen from sobbing. Through an interpreter she told us that she wanted to give her life to God but that years before she had been involved in a number of dark activities. She spoke of being tormented by fear and needing help to be free.

Those of us who joined hands with Lucinda for prayer got a first-hand look at God's marvelous power as He released this woman from her painful captivity. In a matter of minutes she went from being hunched over in agony to standing tall. Although mascara lines streaked her cheeks, her eyes reflected peace.

As I continued musing during my trek down the beach, gentle waves lapped up over my feet, cooling them from the heat of the sun. But for some reason, in spite of the breathtaking beauty around me, my thoughts wandered onto a negative track. The hair-raising close calls we had had in the van a few days before came flooding back. Then thoughts of Nathan's hide-and-seek game intruded, and I fretted over the possibility of it happening again. His vulnerabilities and inability to sense danger scared me. I knew that the others in the family would take good care of him after I left for the women's retreat, but knowing that I wasn't going to be with him during the next couple of days left me feeling as if I had less control.

As my sense of control decreased, my anxiety increased. I fretted and stewed and fretted and stewed, toxic with worry—as if my worry, in some magical way, could prevent a disaster from happening. When you think about it, it's ridiculous. Even though I'd been present with my family, I hadn't had the power to control the things that had evoked my anxiety in the first place.

So I whispered a brief prayer asking God to deliver me from those crazy, pesky fears, just as I had seen Him deliver Lucinda from her turmoil the night before.

During that hour I walked the length of the beach, passing dozens of hotels and establishments that catered to tourists. On my way back down the strip, the thought of a piping hot, fresh-brewed cup of coffee crossed my mind. Noticing a lovely outdoor café at one of the prettiest hotels on the beach, I decided to stop and order some coffee to go. I was in my running gear and had on my baseball cap, sunglasses, and headphones—not exactly the proper attire for the classy restaurant.

When I walked up the steps a young woman greeted me, and I ordered my coffee. She sent a waiter to the kitchen to get it, turned to me, and in accented English asked, "You been out running?"

"Yes," I replied, "but I really walk more than I run."

"So, how far you walk?"

"Oh, about five or six miles," I responded. "It gives me some time to myself."

"You have kids?"

"Yes, I have three children. My husband is with them. They're all still sleeping."

"You a strong woman," she said, catching me a bit off guard.

"Oh—I don't know about that," I said, shaking my head and smiling. "I have days when I don't feel very strong." As those words slipped from my mouth, I felt a blush of embarrassment and wondered why I had said them. I'm usually not that open with strangers.

"No. No. I see God in you. You are strong!" she responded with enthusiasm.

I wondered who in the world this woman was and why she would make such a bold statement to a complete stranger. "Yes, I do have God in my heart. Do you?" I asked, curious where the conversation would lead.

"Oh, *sí, sí, sí!*" she exclaimed.

"Do you have a church that you attend?"

"*Sí, sí. El Centro de Fe.*"

"The Center of Faith?" I asked curiously. "My husband and I were there last night."

It was as if someone had flipped a switch. She lit up from head to toe and asked, "Did you hear the message?"

Taking off my sunglasses and headphones, I smiled and said, "My husband is John, and I'm Pam. We gave the message last night."

I thought the young woman was going to faint from excitement. Her chin almost hit the floor, and she let out a screech that turned several heads in our direction. After she settled down, she introduced herself: "Remember me? I'm Lucinda. I'm the one who is free!"

Lucinda's countenance glowed. She looked so radically different from the night before that I hadn't even recognized her. No more puffy, red eyes. No mascara smudges and smears. No remnants of the agony and pain that had been written across her face. She was electric with joy. She and I chatted for a few minutes about what God had done for her. Then we hugged each other, and I paid for my coffee and left.

Amazing! I thought. *Out of the dozens of hotels on this sandy strip, I "just happened" to ask for a cup of coffee where Lucinda works. Out of the dozens of waiters and waitresses working in the bustling restaurant, Lucinda "just happened" to be the one who walked over to help me.*

Coincidence? I don't think so. I believe it was a divine setup. God wanted me to know that He was leading me. He was directing my plans. He was mindful of my worries and wanted to assure me that He was big enough to take care of every one of them.

The entire way home I kept shaking my head, marveling over God's kindness and gentle love. He knew the heavy anxiety that weighed me down as I walked the beach that morning, and He wanted to send a very clear message: *Pam, would you please relax? Trust Me with your family. I am ordering your steps, even when you aren't aware of it. I am going before you. I am going behind you. Let go of your worries. My intention is to bless you.*

I'm a bit slow to learn at times, but this time I got it. As I sensed God extending His love to me, I relaxed the death grip on my worries and received the peace that He had wanted to give me all along.

How about you? Are you clinging to worries today? All the worrying in the world isn't going to make a positive difference in the outcome of whatever is troubling you. Toxic worry isn't magic; it's misery. It doesn't solve problems; it creates problems. It doesn't provide answers; it scrambles our radar and keeps us from receiving the answers we need.

Hanging on to worry and anxiety won't do you any good. But I know something that will: Relax your grip. *Let go!* Open your hand so that you can receive all that God has in store for you. He loves you. He cares about every last detail of your life. And He is more capable of meeting your deepest needs than anyone else in this universe.

If you're going to cling to something or someone, cling to God. His hand of love is extended to you. He awaits your invitation. Would you like Him to help you conquer your fears? Are you longing for healing and emotional freedom? Do you need God to lead you to paths of peace? If so, take His hand and hang on for all you're worth.

By the way, His companionship comes with a guarantee. When you open your heart to Him, He promises that He will never, ever let go.

Reclaim Your Life

FOOD FOR THOUGHT

For God is greater than our hearts, and he knows everything.

1 JOHN 3:20

PRAYER FOR TODAY

Father, why is it so hard for me to give my agenda to You? Things in my life have not always turned out according to my plans, and it's difficult to realize that You might be working Your will for me through those seemingly unwanted circumstances. Please help me to realize the things I cannot control and to stop wasting energy forcing my agenda. Thank You that when I finally realize this and run to You, I find Your arms open wide to me. What a gift! And I pray that when concerns, fears, or uncertainties plague me, I won't forget those open arms—that You long to hear my cries and care for me. Lord, You are so good. In all these things I praise You. Amen.

STEPS TO TAKE THIS MONTH

- Is it possible you're being cut back right now? Have you known this for some time, or are you just now realizing what God might be doing in your life? Get out your journal and write down your feelings. If you're ready, write a prayer of surrender to God and give Him your agenda.

- "Look instead for what God can do." What situations in your life have you been trying to fix on your own? Has it worked? This month, why not actively look for what God can do in your life and through your difficulties? Let go of those things and run to God—let

Him help you! Perhaps write down those few items on a card and place it on your bathroom mirror or fridge so you'll be reminded daily of God's power in your life.

- Is a "residue of fear" clouding up your outlook? You're not alone! Why not start a prayer journal—a "worry registry." Buy yourself a nice journal that you'll look forward to using and commit to journaling in it daily for a month, releasing your pent-up emotion and open the door to God's intervention. God will bless you so much through this discipline you may even decide to make it a lifelong practice.

- What worries, cares, and problems are you grasping tightly right now? List them on a sheet of paper. Crumple the list tightly in your hand...and then open your hand and let the paper drop to the floor. As you do that, open your heart as well, and let God take these worries from you.

BE AUTHENTIC

❧

A heart at peace gives life to the body.

PROVERBS 14:30

Chapter Ten

RELEASE
YOUR FEELINGS

*Do not let it be imagined that one must remain silent
about one's feelings of rebellion in order to enter into dialogue
with God. Quite the opposite is the truth: it is precisely when
one expresses them that a dialogue of truth begins.*

PAUL TOURNIER

*P*ainful emotions are built into the letting-go process.

No matter what we have to let go of, whether it's sending our youngest off to kindergarten or saying a final good-bye to our spouse of more than fifty years, we will feel grief. We will feel some degree of sadness, ambivalence, emptiness, anger, or confusion. These feelings aren't bad. They're normal, and it's necessary for us to feel them.

Time and again psychiatric research has shown that an important part of letting go is feeling. Feeling leads to release. Denying, stuffing, or numbing our feelings with some sort of addictive behavior only prolongs and intensifies our grief. It blocks us from moving on in life.

I remember the ache in my empty arms after our first baby died halfway to term. As my postpartum hormones raged, the grief was more than I wanted to endure. At the counseling center one morning I said to a colleague, "I wish there were a pill I could take that would make these feelings go away."

He was very kind and, like a good friend, he spoke the truth in love: "I can sure understand that, but then you would just have to work through your grief later."

He was making a point that I understand more fully now: *Letting go demands that we feel and ride out our painful emotions.*

You may not want to hear this, but here it is: When we are feeling our pain, we are progressing. We tend to get mixed up about this process. We think that if we feel pain deeply, we're losing it, cracking up, or getting ready for the funny farm. Nothing is further from the truth. When we are feeling, we are moving ahead through the grief process.

I have a few statements I like to teach my clients:

"Fish swim, birds fly, people feel."

"Feeling is healing."

"We get stuck in our pain not because we don't care, but because we don't give ourselves permission to feel."

In our book *Women and Stress,* Jean Lush and I share sixteen creative ways to release feelings constructively.[4] When we talk about managing emotions, we use a simple diagram of a storage pot. We are all storage pots. Scraps of emotion—anger, jealousy, guilt, fear, joy, sorrow, excitement—are collected in our pots. In the process of letting go, all sorts of emotional scraps pile up in the pot. These scraps create tension. Our emotions are aroused, churning inside, and we begin feeling agitated, troubled, conflicted, tied up in knots, and out of sorts.

In the midst of this agitation, it's important to remember some basic truths of nature. First, tension is energy, and energy will always strive to be discharged. Discharge may come in a variety of ways, depending on our natural predispositions and choices.

Some people are fighters. They rarely close their lids. Whenever they're tense, they immediately unload their tension, regardless of the cost. They act out their emotions. Their rule of thumb is to find inner peace at any price. Fighters feel much better after blowing off steam, even though those around them may end up splattered on the pavement.

Other people are what I call "flighters." They have mastered the skill of sitting on the lid of their emotions. Since the tension isn't discharged outwardly, it gets discharged inwardly. Flighters commonly suffer from psychosomatic illnesses and depression and engage in behaviors like avoidance and procrastination. Their motto is "I must keep peace at any price."

When we have to let go of something important to us, we need to find ways to open some release valves, as we would on a pressure cooker, to let some of our emotional tension out in constructive ways.

One safe place to start is to talk to God—to tell Him about our hurt, our anger, our disappointment, and our sadness. Not for His sake, but for ours. He already knows the secrets of our hearts. Nothing we say could surprise Him.

I'm not talking about prayers consisting of fancy, pious, religious words. I'm talking about authentically sharing our thoughts and feelings with God as we would with our most trusted friend. Whispers in the dark, cries from a lonely heart, sighs of confusion, and fumbling utterances offered to God will find their way to His ears. Some of the best prayers have more feelings than words.

I've seen powerful breakthroughs when people invited the healing presence of God into their places of brokenness. Some of the most effective therapy occurs when people talk to God in prayer. As they share their pain with Him, healing happens. When they have suffered terrible losses and gross injustices, logic and pat answers don't defuse their pain. Releasing their grief does.

I've seen it in my own life. The morning after our son was diagnosed with Down's syndrome, I consulted with a physician in my hospital room. Still reeling from the news of my baby's condition, I looked at the physician and asked, "How did this happen?"

He did what he was supposed to do. He gave me the scientific explanation for Down's syndrome and Nathan's heart problems and tried his best to comfort me. I'll never forget his closing comment: "Mrs. Vredevelt, it was just a chromosomal anomaly, a genetic mishap, *a mistake.*"

I know that the man sincerely felt bad for me and that he wanted to alleviate any guilt I might have felt at the time. The whys of medical crises are sometimes as baffling to doctors as they are to patients. I was grateful for the compassion I saw in his eyes.

But when he left, I didn't know what to do with the information he'd given me.

A mistake? *Whose* mistake?

I propped myself up with a few pillows and sat there in a stupor, overwhelmed by a mishmash of thoughts. Defending myself against the pain, I intellectualized the ordeal. *Okay, Pam, this is how it works. You live in an imperfect world, and your body isn't perfect. Your body made the mistake. Or perhaps the mistake occurred during the process of conception.*

Logic didn't heal the pain. It rarely does.

No, it's when we are open and honest about our thoughts and feelings in safe relationships that healing comes. First Peter 5:7 says, "Cast all your anxiety on him because he cares for you." The word *cast* is a very aggressive term that means "to throw off."

Intellectualizing and using logic as a defense against my pain didn't facilitate healing. It was only as I openly shared my thoughts and feelings with God—and purged the pain in my soul within the safety of His healing presence—that comfort came.

In the Psalms we see that David mastered the art of throwing his pain onto the Lord in prayer. He didn't censor his feelings. He didn't carefully weigh his words. He didn't try to pretend that things were fine when they were awful. Nothing was sugarcoated. David was brutally honest about his feelings as he poured out the depths of his heart to God:

Open your ears, God, to my prayer;
don't pretend you don't hear me knocking.
Come close and whisper your answer.
I really need you....
My insides are turned inside out....
I shake with fear,
I shudder from head to foot.
"Who will give me wings," I ask—
"wings like a dove?"
Get me out of here on dove wings;
I want some peace and quiet....
Haul my betrayers off alive to hell—let them
experience the horror, let them
feel every desolate detail of a damned life.
I call to God;
God will help me.
At dusk, dawn, and noon I sigh
deep sighs—he hears, he rescues....
Pile your troubles on God's shoulders—

he'll carry your load, he'll help you out.
He'll never let good people
topple into ruin. (Psalm 55:1-2, 4-7, 15-17, 22, *The Message*)

That's probably not a prayer you learned at camp or in Sunday school. But maybe it should have been! We grow up learning polite, formal, sanitized prayers—prayers that do us little good when we are plunged into crisis.

Did you know that two-thirds of the Psalms are songs of lament? Time and again we see a pattern in this very human book of poetry: David comes to the Lord in anguish and vents his deepest feelings, but by the end of the psalm, he sees things from a fresh perspective of hope.

Prayers of ventilation will allow you to release your feelings constructively. Journaling can help too. You can write uncensored thoughts, free-flowing feelings, and letters to the Lord about what's going on in your inner world.

And for heaven's sake, give yourself permission to cry!

Don't try to keep a stiff upper lip. God gave us tear ducts for a reason. Tears cleanse the soul. Whenever I counsel grieving people, I encourage them to carve out times when they can have a good, hard cry and express their sadness fully. But I also encourage them to place some limits on that expression. I suggest that after some deep sobbing they make themselves a cup of tea, take a bath, go for a walk, or scrub their kitchen floors to purposely divert themselves from their pain for a while. The key is full expression—within limits.

Why limits? Because we can work ourselves into a neurotic mess if we give full vent to negative feelings for hours at a time. One of the reasons therapy sessions are limited to about fifty minutes is because if they are much longer, clients get weary and recovery work is less than effective. Freedom with containment is the key.

I saw a refreshing authenticity in Nancy as she picked up the pieces of her life after learning of her husband's affair. She had suspected the betrayal for quite some time but discounted the warning signs and shamed herself for being suspicious. His confession blew her world apart. Resentment and bitterness smothered her. She seriously wondered if she would ever be able to dig her way out from under these realities. I'll let Nancy tell her story:

I remember reading the Bible and wondering where God was in this mess. I read stories of God's healing and grace and thought, *What a crock! These words must have been written by people who were out of touch with reality.*

It was hard for me to trust anyone, much less God. I did a fine job of protecting myself from Him and everyone else with a shield of angry detachment. The only one I allowed anywhere near my heart was my best friend, Karen.

Karen stayed close in this dark valley. She prayed for me each day. She talked about God's love and about her high hopes for my future. She listened to me. She cried with me. She did not judge me. And she didn't tell me what to do.

During our separation, Doug visited the children periodically for a few hours at a time. Our kids were broken by the sorrow of our fragmented marriage and the uncertainty of the ongoing separation. I was barely able to function under the stress of the changes. I think the only reason I kept going was because I felt the deep need to relieve the children's pain. It was strictly for their sake that I reached out to others and persevered.

These were dark years that caused me to take inventory. I

took a long, hard look at me. I remember crying in a heap on the bathroom floor, asking God to change me. I begged Him for strength to cope with the bone-crushing weariness that came from my unrelenting efforts to hold our family together. Eventually the blinders were lifted from my eyes, and I could see that I was absolutely powerless over Doug's choices.

I also asked God to heal the pervasive suspicion and fear that had consumed me. Healing began when I was completely honest and said, *God, I don't trust You, but I see people who do and I want to.* Even though fear distorted my picture of reality, I knew deep down that God was the only one who had the answers that I could not find within myself.

For several years, though, it seemed as if I had lost my way with God. I continued to wonder if there was something terribly wrong with me and if somehow Doug was justified in his choices. I filed for divorce and remained silent about Doug's infidelity. People questioned me. They asked why I couldn't forgive him. Surely, they thought, we could have worked things out.

But they didn't know the whole story, and, frankly, I didn't think it was any of their business. Trying my best to go on without Doug, I slammed the door shut on the guilt over filing for divorce and the unresolved grief over losing our family.

I had long, angry talks with God. I raged. I asked Him where He was when my husband was betraying me. Why hadn't He protected me and the children from this abuse? I told Him how desperately unsafe I felt in this God-forsaken world. I wondered about the next shoe He planned to drop.

All the while, God listened patiently and continued

sending blessings that were difficult for me to see through the dense fog of my grief.

I was so overcome with the injustice the children and I had suffered that I wanted Doug to pay. Vengeance seemed like a practical and logical solution. If I just opened my mouth and told all, I could have destroyed him.

But something constrained me. Actually, Someone constrained me. The Spirit of God began to speak to me about letting go of my bitterness. Everywhere I turned, somebody was saying something about forgiveness. The lady on *The Oprah Winfrey Show*. The song on the radio. The preacher at church. My friend on the phone. They were all delivering the same message: "Forgive."

Forgive? I cried to God. *Impossible! How do you forgive people who don't deserve forgiveness?*

"You pray for them."

But, God, I don't want to pray for Doug. I don't want to pray for his sideline attractions. They betrayed me. I will hate them forever!

"Not if you pray for them."

It was about the time that this war was going on in my head that Karen gave me Dr. James Dobson's book *When God Doesn't Make Sense,* which explores the subject of suffering unjustly. As I read, the doctor brought me face-to-face with a set of choices. I could either continue my descent into bitterness and resentment, or I could turn to God. Neither choice seemed very appealing.

I wrestled with these ideas for months before I was able to bring myself to tell God that I couldn't let go on my own. A gratifying sense of power came from holding on to my anger and resentment. There was a part of me that wondered if I would crumble if I released it. I needed God to give me supernatural strength to do what He had asked me to do: pray for those who had betrayed me.

Moments of fleeting relief came as I journaled my uncensored feelings in a daily diary. Revealing the most intimate details of my life helped purge the pain. I read about a man named Job who was able to put words to the anguish I was feeling. I found solace in his life story and in the fact that God was the one who had the final word in his life. Not his friends. Not his family. Not his acquaintances. It gave me hope to know that God's last word in Job's life was one of total restoration.

It is true that the injustices I suffered from my husband's sexual addiction stole my sense of worth and personal dignity. But, looking back, I can see that the bitterness I hung on to for several years robbed me of the ability to heal and move forward. A turning point came when I realized that I could not afford to leave unchecked the hatred simmering in my heart.

I had to acknowledge that what happened to me *happened*. I was not crazy. My children and I bore the scars of a terrible injustice. But denial was not the answer. Neither was amnesia or sugarcoating the truth. I had to face the facts and grieve the reality of the injustice if I was ever going to be able to move beyond it. I knew I couldn't keep trying to cover the cracks in my heart for the rest of my life.

Somewhere along the line, I heard someone say that if we all lived by the rule "an eye for an eye," the whole world would be blind. It reminded me of the many mistakes I had made in my life and of God's unending compassion and grace to forgive me. How could I not forgive when God had forgiven me of so much? I made a conscious choice to let go of my quest for justice for Doug and the women who had betrayed me.

I felt nothing. But I did what I knew God had told me to do months before. I prayed for them and released them into God's hands. I decided that from that day forward it wasn't my job to set them straight or to make them pay. Their wrongs were between them and God. My energies were going to be focused on my own health and the well-being of my children.

To this day I have moments when the past, with all of its hurts and memories of failure, sweeps in like a raging river and leaves me gasping for air. I visit the pain every so often, but I no longer live in it. I am now one of those stories of hope that I used to read about while consumed with anger.

I'm convinced that nothing will kill a woman's spirit faster than holding on to resentment. And nothing will dissolve bitterness more effectively than choosing to let go and forgive. Forgiveness doesn't come easily, and believing it does will likely ensure that we never forgive. If we call a spade a spade, forgiveness is often unattainable from a human standpoint. But when you factor in the divine, all things are possible. God can supernaturally empower us to release our death grip on rage and let it go. We simply have to say, *God, I'm willing to be made willing.*

I told the Lord several years ago that I was willing. And from then on I began to sense that God was touched by my pain, that He had taken up my cause, and that He held both me and Doug in His hands. He would have the final say in both of our lives. Eventually I embraced the peace that only God could give. The pain of abandonment will probably never go away, because we suffered many severe losses. But the girls and I have moved on with our lives, and while we grieve our losses, we are no longer controlled by them. There is life beyond Doug. And it's a good life, blessed by God.

If we want to snip the soul ties that keep us in bondage…
If we want to take back the dignity that has been stolen from us…
If we want God to heal the holes in our souls…
If we want to douse the flames of bitter revenge…
If we want something good to come out of something very, very bad…
…we must take the steps of healing.

We must recognize that what is, *is* and not avoid or rationalize away our losses. We must relinquish control to God with full awareness that He is God and we are not. And we must experience and release our feelings. Feeling is healing.

Life requires us to let go over and over and over again. Letting go doesn't eliminate our loss, but it reduces unnecessary suffering. As we do our part, God will *always* do His. When we release our grip and open our hands to Him, we give Him a new place to deposit whatever we need to move us forward in our healing.

Chapter Eleven

REACH OUT

The deepest need of man is the need to overcome
his separateness, to leave the prison of his aloneness.

ERICH FROMM

*M*edical professionals have told me that people who suffer chest pain typically seek medical assistance within a week. That's a fairly quick response time. Did you know that the average time it takes a married couple to seek assistance when they are suffering pain in their relationship is not six days, six weeks, or even six months?

Try six years!

No wonder the divorce statistics are off the charts. Why are we more apt to ask for help with physical pain than emotional pain? I'm not sure. But one thing is certain: The results are devastating, and most of us endure a lot of unnecessary suffering.

This is not God's plan for us. Everything about God is relational. From the very beginning of time, He designed us to enjoy intimate relationships with Him and others. He longs to walk arm-in-arm with us—and to provide empathetic friends and helpers to walk with us—through the sorrows and sufferings that are an inevitable part of life in this world.

Connections matter. When we withdraw, detach, or close God and others out of our suffering, we cut off our source of life and derail our own healing. The bottom line is that God never intended for us to try to handle our worries and anxieties alone. Peace comes in the context of relationships.

God knows our propensity to fear and discouragement, and He wants us to experience His comfort in the midst of our troubles. One of His names is "The God of All Comfort." The word *comfort,* which is mentioned fifty-nine times in the New Testament, literally means "to call near." It evokes a picture of one person calling out to another to come stand alongside him or her. Comfort comes as we risk reaching out, transparent in our pain, and allow others to come near and strengthen us in our troubled state.

I recall a final counseling session with a woman I treated for an anxiety disorder after she had a radical mastectomy. After several months of therapy, during which she grieved her losses, established new goals, and tried a variety of medications before finding the right fit, she was ready to put closure on counseling.

I'll never forget her final remark. With tears in her eyes, she grasped my hands tightly and said, "Thank you for befriending my pain."

It had indeed been my privilege. Witnessing her progress spoke volumes to me about the healing power of connecting with safe people to whom we can disclose our deepest conflicts.

As a professional therapist I spend a lot of time with people in their pain. They need someone to help them sort through their confusion, respond to their suffering, help them get unstuck when they become arrested by grief, and strengthen their will to live when they have been diminished by the cruelties of life. They need someone to validate their afflictions and create a safe place for them to process their pain and let it go. Whether or not a specific problem is solved during a counseling session is sometimes irrelevant. Many issues are not resolved quickly. But healing often happens when a person shares his or her suffering with someone safe.

A few months after our nation was attacked by terrorists on September 11, I was invited by the Department of Human Resources in New York City to speak to airline personnel who had lost their jobs and their loved ones on that terrible day. We explored the realities of their post traumatic stress and considered ways to cope with the emotional impact of their losses.

On the way from that event to a television studio, the cab driver asked me why I was in New York. He was a kind gentleman from South Africa who had relocated to America six years before.

I talked about helping people who were struggling with difficult anxieties and post traumatic stress. He listened politely and in the middle of the conversation said, "Lady, I have a hunch."

"A hunch? What kind of a hunch?"

"I have a hunch as to why people are so stressed out."

"I'm all ears. What's your hunch?"

"It's a simple observation," he continued. "In my country, when we are worried or troubled about something we go to a brother. We cry on our brother's shoulder. We tell them our troubles and then we feel better. In America it's very different. People think they should do everything on their own. Independence is number one and people suffer because of it."

I nodded and thought, *He said it like it is.*

Peace and healing come in the context of relationships, not in isolation.

I recall an occasion, years ago, when I was overcome with worry. Despite using all the anxiety-reduction tricks I knew, I was unable to shake the fear. It all started with a letter.

After our first baby died in the womb, I wrote *Empty Arms:*

Emotional Support for Those Who Have Suffered Miscarriage, Stillbirth, or Tubal Pregnancy to encourage others who were suffering similar losses. Cards and letters poured in from women across the country, thanking me for the book and telling me their own stories of loss.

Four weeks prior to delivering our second baby, I received a letter from a woman who found out during her eight-month exam that her baby had died. The doctor had been unable to detect a heartbeat. The details of her story were nearly identical to our experience with our first baby. As I read her letter, all of the memories of our loss came flooding back like a tidal wave.

I tried everything I knew to quiet my fears. I prayed. I sang. I used thought-stopping methods. I scrubbed the kitchen floor. I tried reading my Bible and some other good books. But the anxiety continued. My imagination was toxic with worry.

Not wanting to burden my husband or evoke any unnecessary fear in him, I carried the anxiety alone. That, by the way, was not a smart move. If there is one thing I learned from that incident, it was this: *Never worry alone!*

The next day at our Sunday morning church service, I asked to talk with our pastor's wife. Even though she and her husband were new to our congregation and I didn't know her well, I felt I could trust her.

"I am riddled with worry," I told her. "I received this letter...and I'm afraid the same thing is going to happen all over again." I knew that the anxiety was irrational. There was no evidence that the baby I carried was in danger. But I also realized that I was powerless to find relief on my own.

Diane listened attentively, and I could tell from her responses that she empathized with my struggle. We joined hands, and she prayed for me and for the baby. Although that connection took only five brief minutes, it brought great relief. Peace went home with me that day. Healing happened as we connected with God and with each other.

When I think back over the times in my life when I was overwhelmed by worry and anxiety, I realize that the greatest moments of relief came when I sensed that God and a trusted friend were truly present with me in my struggle. It was as if they opened the door, walked into my turmoil, sat down with me, and, with full acceptance, waited. My brokenness was our meeting place. Inner peace and healing were born within that connection. Their companionship in my suffering brought relief, even though the circumstances that brought about the distress remained the same.

I have learned that whatever we deny, repress, or hide in the dark cannot be healed, but that sharing our concerns openly and exposing them to the light can lead to growth and peace. When your emotional pain seems overwhelming, please resist the temptation to isolate yourself, withdraw, and shrink back in the shadows.

Consider carefully those to whom you can turn for support. Will they listen well? Do they have experience with whatever is troubling you? Do you know that they have your very best interests at heart? Do they have a track record of integrity? Are they healthy enough to offer suggestions and then give you the freedom to make your own decisions?

If so, reach out. It usually takes more than one pair of hands to peel your death grip off your concerns.

So you can let them go.

Reclaim Your Life

FOOD FOR THOUGHT

> {The Lord said,} "Be strong and courageous.
> Do not be terrified; do not be discouraged, for the LORD
> your God will be with you wherever you go."

JOSHUA 1:9

PRAYER FOR TODAY

Dear God, I have let anxieties rule my life for too long. I want to place all of it at Your throne. Thank You for being the best friend I could ever hope for, for listening and loving like no other. I've tried for too long to manage all of this on my own, and it's not working. Lord, I release it all to you. When I'm getting ready to fight or fly or do it on my own, please tug at my heart and draw me to You. And, in the process, please help me to think about the others around me and the joys you bring to my life daily. I thank You for all those gifts. In Your name I pray, amen.

STEPS TO TAKE THIS MONTH

- Whether you're a fighter or a "flighter," use the tools from chapter 10 to learn to release your feelings in a constructive way. Begin by talking to God—He is the best confidant you will ever find. You may want to record your prayers, as well as God's answers, in a journal.

- Are you struggling alone with anxieties and fears? Why? Be honest with yourself and acknowledge the ways you've pulled away. Where can you find places to reconnect? Friendships you've neglected, church fellowship, areas where you can serve? Ask God to help you reestablish connections in your life.

GIVE YOURSELF GRACE

~

*The knowledge that we are never alone
calms the troubled sea of our lives and
speaks peace to our souls.*

A. W. TOZER

Chapter Twelve

REVISIT
THE BASICS

Renewal and restoration are not luxuries.
They are essentials. There is absolutely nothing enviable
or spiritual about a coronary or a nervous breakdown, nor is
an ultra-busy schedule necessarily the mark of a productive life.

CHUCK SWINDOLL

I buckled myself into the seat, glanced out the window of the plane, and checked my watch. *So far, so good.* We were departing on schedule. The flight attendant welcomed us aboard and gave the usual instructions: "In the event that the cabin loses pressure, an oxygen mask will fall from the compartment above you. Slip the mask over your nose and mouth and breathe normally. If you are traveling with children or someone is seated next to you who needs help, put your own mask on first and then help others."

I had heard the statement hundreds of times before, but this time something about it struck a dissonant chord in me. The thought crossed my mind that my natural reaction would be to want to help my children first. No doubt that's why they give the instructions. The authorities are well aware of a parent's instinct to protect, and they also know that a child requires less oxygen than an adult. If adults pass out from oxygen deprivation, they aren't going to be of any help to children.

Now and then I observe a paradox among those who serve others: caretakers who don't take care of themselves. Many people I talk with in my counseling office or at conferences regularly place their own needs at the bottom of their to-do lists. The job, the boss, the kids, the spouse, the community, the church—everyone else gets the best they have to offer. The caretakers get the leftovers, as if everyone's life except theirs deserves attention and support. The tragic result is that these caring folks end up living life on the verge of burnout.

While talking with Carmen during a therapy session, I learned that she had been the primary caretaker of her ailing parents for ten years. She nursed her father for four years before he died. Shortly after he passed on, her mother had a stroke, and Carmen spent the next six years attending to her needs.

Not surprisingly, after her mother's death, Carmen felt like she was "caving in." The loss of her beloved parents was intensely painful, but exhaustion further complicated the grief. When I asked Carmen about the nature of some of her own needs, her eyes glazed over into a blank stare. "I don't know," she sighed. "I really haven't thought about it." Together we set out to help her think about it and learn the basics of healthy self-care.

Grief is hard work. It takes emotional energy to let go of something near and dear to our hearts. When we're processing a painful loss, it's important to give ourselves permission to downshift into survival mode, to streamline our activities and conserve our mental and emotional resources. We typically don't have much of an emotional buffer when we're in the throes of a major life adjustment.

That's why self-care is critically important.

Revisiting the basics is a good place to start. It's amazing how symptoms of anxiety and depression are diminished by incorporating three simple ingredients into our routines: healthy meals, ample sleep, and regular exercise. They provide a firm foundation for successfully letting go. If we subtract one or more of these three components from the equation, we run the risk of arresting, or at least inhibiting, our forward movement in life.

Think about it. Have you ever noticed that when you are in a time of transition, your eating, sleeping, and exercise habits tend to become somewhat erratic? Transitions are stressful. When stress increases, compulsions also increase, and routine tends to be less than consistent. We find ourselves eating more (or less) than necessary, grabbing junk food on the run, or skipping meals altogether. Our sleep patterns can become erratic. We may sleep more than usual, lie awake at night, or burn the candle at both ends. Likewise, we may cut back on exercise, skip it altogether, or become more compulsive about it.

Let's revisit these basics, one by one, and examine ways to manage them during the letting-go process.

DAILY BREAD

There are many helpful books that offer sound eating programs, so I don't want to go into great detail here, but I do want to underline the importance of consistently eating nutritious food. For some that means three balanced meals a day. For others, depending on their energy output and blood-sugar sensitivities, it may mean four or five small meals a day.

During a season of letting go, what you eat can make a significant difference in your endurance. Letting go of disappointment and painful losses requires high-octane fuel. Diet soda and junk food aren't going to give you what you need when you're mentally and emotionally taxed by chronic stress. Some nutritional experts suggest increasing your protein intake at such times, because protein is a stabilizing energy source that burns longer than carbohydrates. Adding a high-quality vitamin-mineral supplement can also bolster the body during prolonged periods of stress.

In the year following Nathan's birth, I was physically and mentally exhausted from adjusting to the reality of his handicaps, illnesses, sleepless nights, and the fluctuating hormones in my postpartum body.

I had to *force* myself to eat three healthy meals a day.

Since I had no creative energy for cooking fancy meals, I had to simplify everything. The objective was to get something from each of the five food groups (meat, dairy, fruit, vegetable, and starch) every meal. I relied on simple cuts of meat, convenience foods, and recipes that were quick and easy to prepare. During that year we barbecued on the gas grill several times a week and frequently used the rice cooker. Fruit, nuts, and protein bars provided quick, energy-boosting snacks between meals.

While I'm sure there were days when I didn't hit my objective, at least I had a target to shoot at. Remember the old saying: If you aim at nothing, you're sure to hit it. On days when I was more disciplined and stuck with the program, my stamina was significantly better, and there was a marked difference in my emotional energy.

DAILY REST

Sleep is another of our most important needs when we're in the process of letting go. I remember talking with a mother whose eleven-month-old baby had died after complications from surgery.

"All I want to do is sleep," she complained.

While it's a fact that one of the red flags of depression is wanting to sleep more than necessary, I was puzzled by her remark. After her baby died, she had taken a full-time job and was putting in ten-hour days as an executive assistant. I asked her how much she slept, and she said, "From 9 p.m. to 7 a.m.," as if this were a ridiculous amount of time to be in bed.

It had never crossed this woman's mind that she *needed* the extra sleep because of the heavy emotional burden she was bearing—not to mention the stress of learning a new job! From my perspective, those ten hours of sleep didn't point to pathology; they indicated good self-care. The body needs time to restore and replenish itself when we are carrying heavy emotional loads.

"For those who are suffering with symptoms of anxiety and depression, I'm going to save you $120 right now," I said to a group of professionals gathered for a stress-management conference. "You can significantly reduce these symptoms by getting eight to nine hours of sleep a night."

As I expected, people fidgeted in their seats, smirked, glanced around, and gave me *the look*. You know, the look that says, "Yeah, right, lady! What planet do you live on?" Of the several hundred gathered in the room that day, very few raised their hands when I asked, "Who averages eight to nine hours of sleep a night?"

We live in a fast-paced world, constantly struggling to meet its unending demands. We work, raise families, build marriages, tend to friendships, and try to cram in some exercise and recreational activities. Our daily planners are full of to-do lists. There are never enough hours in a day to get it all done.

A friend of mine recently had his gall bladder removed. As a corporate executive, he was used to having a lot of energy and maintaining a high level of productivity, but recuperating was taking its toll. When he complained to his doctor that he was still feeling tired two weeks after the surgery, his doctor said, "Following this type of surgery, the body heals at a rate of 45 percent per month from the inside out—*if* a person rests and takes good care of himself. If you push too hard, you'll delay your recovery."

When we suffer a major disappointment or a difficult loss, it's as if part of who we are is surgically severed or cut away. It takes time and rest to recover. Sleep is one of the primary ways the body restores itself. If we rob ourselves of it through overactivity, we slow our recovery and impair the healing process. In short, we prolong and intensify the pain involved in letting go.

My grandfather, an entrepreneur and a successful businessman, used to say, "The only problem with sleep is that you've got to take it lying down." He was a hard-working man who could close his eyes and catch a few winks just about anywhere and then awake refreshed for the rest of the day. These catnaps were in addition to the solid eight hours of sleep he got at night. It's a model of self-care worth considering.

We're more likely to be successful in our endeavors of letting go if we lay aside our to-do lists and put ourselves to bed in a timely fashion. With refreshed minds and healthy bodies, we'll be more effective in handling the new list tomorrow.

DAILY EXERCISE

Finally, when you're doing the hard work of letting go, exercise is prescriptive, not optional. Although I'm not an expert in physiology, as a clinical counselor I know the mental and emotional benefits of exercise. Studies have shown that exercise is a key to managing depression and anxiety. It's a cheap, easy way to elevate mood, decrease agitation, and deliver a sense of calm to the brain. The endorphins released during aerobic exercise, for example, are powerful mood elevators and natural tranquilizers. Exercise is also a superb tool for managing anger. When we exercise, we physically force tension out of our bodies.

For as long as I can remember, exercise has been a part of my routine. I used to swim a mile on my lunch hour. After my children were born, I had less time and energy for the pool routine, so I started walking—something I still do today.

When the weather is nice, I enjoy walking the hills in our neighborhood for thirty to sixty minutes, four or five days a week. If it's pouring rain, a treadmill comes in handy. While I do have to carve out time in my schedule for walking, I think I probably save time in the long run. My proficiency on tasks is much better when my mood is good, my mind peaceful, and my body strong. The more hectic and pressured a week becomes, the more I need my "sanity walk" to defuse the tension, restore calm, and help me sleep deeply at night.

The most frequent rebuttal I hear to the argument for exercise is that it just takes too much time. But exercise for enhancing our emotional state really requires only thirty to forty minutes, several times a week. We don't have to spend long hours in the gym. Some experts say that maintaining a consistent training-level heart rate for twenty-five minutes will alter the brain chemistry in much the same way that an antidepressant does.

I encourage my clients to set aside a minimum of thirty minutes for any aerobic activity, since it takes a few minutes to work the heart up to a training-level pulse. An exercise trainer at a local club can help you calculate your training heart rate based on your age and overall physical condition.

For me, the benefits far outweigh the costs. In fact, when I don't exercise, I pay for it. I'm more irritable, little things get to me, and I find myself reacting to life in ways I don't want to.

If you are in the middle of transition, struggling emotionally with deep disappointment or painful loss, I sincerely hope you will set aside time for exercise. It really doesn't matter what kind of activity you choose, as long as it's aerobic and increases your heart rate and the flow of oxygen and blood to the brain. Do something you enjoy. Walk. Ride a bike. Swim. Jog. Rollerblade. Play an intense game of basketball. Any activity is worthwhile if it pushes the tension out of your body and releases the natural chemicals in the brain that help you cope.

When we are doing the hard work of letting go, we can assist the process by downshifting into survival mode and getting back to the basics. Taking care of ourselves isn't selfish—it's smart. If we are tending to our own needs, we are more likely to have something worthwhile to offer others. Jesus said, "Love your neighbor as yourself" (Luke 10:27). Our effectiveness in loving others begins with a choice to love ourselves. When we fill ourselves up first, we're more likely to have something worthwhile to pass on to another.

As every flight attendant reminds us, it's impossible to offer others oxygen if we've ceased breathing ourselves.

Chapter Thirteen

REMEMBER

Remember that nothing is going to happen
to you today that you and God cannot handle together.

I've noticed something about myself and people in general:
When we are sad, discouraged, afraid, or angry, our thoughts
can easily wander onto a negative track. Grief distorts our perceptions. Emotional pain fuels faulty thinking and can bring on crises of
faith. Pain skews judgment and can cause us to view reality with a
pessimistic eye.

On the other hand, deliberately recalling God's goodness can
lead us out of our discouraging doldrums. It's a good life strategy.
That's what David, the writer of many of the Psalms, did when he
was worn so thin that he didn't know if he could face another day in
this world.

David, a man with a big heart and a tall assignment, knew well
the highs and lows that come with life. His words reflect the anguish
of his soul:

I cry to the Lord; I call and call to him. Oh, that he would
listen. I am in deep trouble and I need his help so badly. All
night long I pray, lifting my hands to heaven, pleading.
There can be no joy for me until he acts. I think of God and

moan, overwhelmed with longing for his help. I cannot sleep until you act. I am too distressed even to pray!

Has the Lord rejected me forever? Will he never again be favorable? Is his lovingkindness gone forever? Has his promise failed? Has he forgotten to be kind to one so undeserving? Has he slammed the door in anger on his love? And I said: This is my fate, that the blessings of God have changed to hate. (Psalm 77:1-4, 7-10, TLB)

But as we read further in the Psalm, something in David's mood and tone does an about-face. Suddenly a song of praise bubbles from the depths of his dark pool of despair:

O God, your ways are holy. Where is there any other as mighty as you? You are the God of miracles and wonders! You still demonstrate your awesome power. (vv. 13-14, TLB)

What made the difference? What brought about the change in David's heart? What washed away his grief? Sandwiched between verses 10 and 13 is the key—the passage in which David pauses and remembers. Here he recounts God's faithful acts of love in his past:

I recall the many miracles he did for me so long ago. Those wonderful deeds are constantly in my thoughts. I cannot stop thinking about them. (vv. 11-12, TLB)

How about you? What do you do in those times of life when you're so beaten down by demands that you're too tired to pray? (By the way, lest you think you're all alone, I haven't yet met a person who hasn't been there, including the woman I see in the mirror every day!) What do you do when you feel as though you're at the end of your rope and there's simply not enough strength to keep holding on? What do you do when it seems that the entire world is fighting against you?

David did something helpful. And simple. And very effective.

He remembered.

The son of Jesse listed all the times when God had made a difference in his past.

Everyone has experienced God's loving activity at a pivotal moment in his or her life. I've had those moments. You've had those moments. We may not have recognized them every time, but God has been actively involved in our lives from day one.

Think about it. Have you ever had a narrow escape from a tough situation and felt that an invisible bodyguard had protected you? Have you considered the possibility that God was the one who rescued you?

Have you ever received a blessing you know you didn't earn? God is the giver of all good gifts.

Have you ever steered away from trouble and toward something more noble because something inside you quietly craved purity? Only God makes people want to be holy.

Have you ever made a good decision that took you in a surprisingly positive direction just because you felt "led"? My hunch is that God was speaking to you.

Have you ever gone through a hard time, only to discover later that those difficult circumstances prepared you for something greater in your life? God is good at bringing something of great value out of adversity.

Many of us have probably discounted moments like these and considered them coincidence, luck, or a fluke. Or perhaps we celebrated some of these divine interventions but lost sight of them in the fog of the daily grind of life. The real question is not whether we've had moments when God intervened in our lives. The question is: What have we done with them?[4]

Remembering God's presence with me in the past gives me the faith and courage to handle the situations I face now. But how easy it is to forget! The memory dulls. We go to retrieve something from our mental files only to find the cabinet locked.

Yet we *must* remember, because memories can beef up our courage. For years I've used the technique of recalling positive memories to empower my clients for peak performance. I've worked with a number of top collegiate athletes who struggle with anxiety, depression, and eating disorders. They need to prepare themselves mentally to compete, and as they anticipate an upcoming event they have a choice. They can rehearse the times in their pasts when they made mistakes or major blunders and fell apart under pressure, or they can recall the times when they operated at their optimal levels. Which memories do you think have the ability to spur them to success?

If recalling positive memories enhances the performance of an athlete facing a challenging competition, imagine the difference it can make in building our faith for managing today's pressures and tomorrow's deadlines.

It seems so simple. I suppose it is. Perhaps we try to make life too complicated and the solutions too difficult.

I think that, in some ways, our spiritual lives become dwarfed when we forget our pasts. There is a propensity in our high-pressured, fast-paced society to allow the urgent demands of today and the worries of tomorrow to dominate our thinking. We live in the information age, and it's easy to jump to the conclusion that if we just gather more facts, secure more data, or run tighter calculations, our problems will be solved. But there comes a time when we need to stop seeking more information or advice and make remembering our prescription of choice.

When Nathan was born with Down's syndrome, John and I went through a deep grieving process. We gathered information about the diagnosis, read book after book, and talked with specialist after specialist. We wanted to understand our son's condition to the best of our ability.

But stockpiling information didn't heal our pain. In fact, there were times when we didn't want to read another word or hear another thing from anyone about Down's syndrome, because the information that increased our awareness also fueled our fears. When we thought about our future of raising a mentally retarded son, we needed more than information. We needed some real-life, rock-solid reminders that God had not abandoned us. We needed some tangible reasons to hope.

That's what remembering gives us.

Doesn't it make sense to build your faith on what you *do* know rather than on what you *don't* know? There are a lot of things I don't know. I don't know why Nathan was born with Down's syndrome. I don't know why he hasn't been able to learn to talk. I don't know whether or not he will ever have the capacity to live and work on his own. Only time will tell. And I could spend a lot of time focusing on all the things I don't know and watch my faith erode. Or I can spend my time rehearsing what I know for sure.

I do know that God loves Nathan and has a plan and purpose for his life. I do know that Nathan has gifts and abilities that are allowing him to make valuable contributions to this world. I do know that while there are many difficulties and sorrows inherent in raising a child with a handicap, there are also many joys. Nathan is teaching us lessons about life and love that we probably would not have learned without him in our family.

How about you? What truths do your stories tell? When did God intervene in your past and help you survive losses and disappointments? If you need help remembering, just ask God. He can open your eyes and help you see a bigger picture.

Jesus said, "The Counselor, the Holy Spirit, whom the Father will send in my name, will teach you all things and will *remind* you of everything I have said to you" (John 14:26).

Why? Because when our hearts are burdened and we need encouragement, remembering matters.

Recalling empowers us.

Reflecting energizes us.

Reminiscing refreshes our spirits, restores our sense of balance...and allows us to let go of our pain.

Chapter Fourteen

REDUCE
STIMULATION

Only in a quiet mind is adequate perception of the world.

HANS MARGOLIUS

I was sick with the flu, laid out flat in bed. My stomach was sour, my body ached, and I felt downright awful. I tried to prop myself up to read, but my head started spinning, and my eyes didn't want to focus on the words in front of me. Setting the book aside, I resumed a horizontal position, grabbed the remote, and flipped on the TV. The morning news was in full swing, and I figured a little diversion from my aches and pains would help.

Ten minutes later I felt worse. The news anchors bombarded me with one horrific story after another. Shooting here. Major car wreck there. Earthquake here. Plane crash there. Robbery here. Lead poisoning and cancer-causing agents there.

One thing's for sure: The media work hard to emotionally hook the viewing audience. They love to hype tragedies and deliver stories with intense emotional impact. The more traumatic the event and sensational the commentary, the better. *Enough already!* The program created more anxiety than it was worth. I turned off the television, threw the covers over my head, and decided to sleep things off.

When you're enduring a stressful time in life, your emotions already tend to be more "charged" than they are when life is going smoothly. Your nerves might feel raw. Adding more negative stimulation to the equation is not going to lead you to inner peace. If you find yourself struggling with worry and anxiety, you might want to evaluate the sources of stimulation you are exposed to on a regular basis. Some of these sources may be intensifying your agitation.

For the first few months following the death of our first baby, I was emotionally ravaged by grief and worried that we wouldn't be able to have children. The stress of the loss and the hormonal changes in my body left me feeling very fragile. Prior to the loss of our baby, my husband and I had routinely read the newspaper in the morning before work and watched the news at the end of the day. After the baby died, though, I couldn't watch movies, listen to songs, or sit through television programs heavily laden with intense emotional content. The excessive stimulation tied my stomach in knots. I simply did not have the emotional stamina to metabolize that much bad news all at once.

Grief has a way of distorting our perceptions. Everything already seems bad, and piling more bad on top of what already seems bad just makes us feel worse.

For several months I carefully selected what I listened to, read, and viewed. I skipped the newspaper and chose more uplifting reading material. Though I didn't like the idea of being less in touch with what was going on in the world, I did enjoy more peace of mind. Instrumental music with soothing harmonies also had a calming effect on my emotions.

Positive input from the outside helped to calm my turmoil on the inside and fortified me to do the grief work I needed to do. These simple adjustments didn't remove the pain of our loss, but they shielded me from additional emotional drain.

As I've worked with people in my counseling office during the last decade, I've noticed a new trend that has the potential of perpetuating anxiety. More and more I'm meeting clients who spend the entire evening after work, or after the kids are in bed, on the Internet.

For those who are somewhat socially anxious, being online can seem a safer place to interact with others. There is no face-to-face contact, and if they don't want to continue interacting with someone, they can click off-line with one push of a button.

Please don't get me wrong. I use the Internet regularly for a variety of purposes. It's a wonderful tool. But problems arise when the 'Net becomes a person's main source of relationship or when the stimulating impact of the activity robs him or her of sleep or interaction with family members and friends.

Virtual friendships cannot meet our needs for healthy human connection because much of what is perceived online is only a small portion of reality—the reality the other person wants you to see in the written word—not the complete picture of who he or she actually is.

I've met men and women who were duped into thinking they had met Prince Charming or Miss Perfect in chat rooms online. It was a heartbreaking and rude awakening when they eventually found out that they had wasted hours, even months, of their lives on some fanciful illusion presented in text. Worse yet, I've talked with clients who unwittingly interacted with smooth-talking users and abusers. What started as an innocent conversation in a chat room led to a scary and troublesome series of events.

I don't want to be a gloom-and-doomer, but I do want to suggest exercising healthy caution and setting time limits for online interactions.

Research supports the importance of using the Internet wisely. I recently read a study funded by a group of computer companies. Researchers went to a town in Pennsylvania and selected two thousand homes that did not have Internet access. The families who agreed to participate in the study were given a computer and Internet access in exchange for the researchers' right to study them for two years.

At the beginning and end of the test period the participants took a psychological test. I don't think the computer companies expected the results they received. At the end of two years the study revealed that those individuals who spent more than one hour online per day were significantly more depressed than before they had access to the Internet.[4]

We don't have to take an all-or-nothing approach. Balance is the key. When we're living with a heightened sense of anxiety, we need to take inventory of what is assaulting our senses. Sometimes we use the media and computers as diversions to escape from our worries. But if we are being bombarded with toxic and emotionally intense messages, or if the time we spend in these activities is robbing us of needed rest or time with loved ones, we might actually be making our problems worse.

A wise old sage by the name of Peter once wrote, "Whoever would love life and see good days...must seek peace and pursue it" (1 Peter 3:10–11). Are you up for a challenge? Even small adjustments that reduce stimulation can have a positive emotional impact and diminish your worries. Why not give it a try? Quiet some of that outside noise for a week or two and see if your world seems like a more enjoyable place to live. See if peace doesn't follow your pursuit and help you let go of some of your anxiety.

Chapter Fifteen

ROCK WITH LAUGHTER

Laugh out loud.
It helps flush out the nervous system.

CHARLES SWINDOLL

When was the last time you had a good, solid belly laugh–you know, the kind that leaves you gasping for air? Did you know that laughter is a medicine for the soul? It can promote sound mental and physical health, deflect anxious thoughts, and help us cope more effectively with overwhelming pressures. Laughter has an amazing power to balance our steps as we walk the tightrope of life.

Medical researchers have discovered that laughter actually stimulates the immune system. It also increases our oxygen intake, lowers blood pressure, and releases endorphins in the pleasure center of the brain, giving us an emotional lift or a natural high, regardless of whatever anxiety-producing circumstances we may be enduring.

My friend Bonnie Kopp recently endured a year filled with the natural worry and anxiety that accompanies a diagnosis of breast cancer. But in the midst of some very long and trying months, Bonnie and her twin sister, Connie Griffith, decided to have some fun.

During their teenage years, Bonnie and Connie were known for pulling "twin switches": On double dates they would swap clothes midway through the evening and pretend to be each other. Even their boyfriends couldn't tell them apart! Now in their fifties, the twins continue their humorous shenanigans. After a visit from this dynamic duo, the radiology lab at Emanuel Hospital has never been the same. I'm going to let Bonnie tell you the story firsthand.

After I was diagnosed with breast cancer, I received radiation treatment five days a week for six weeks. About midway through the process, Connie called to say that she was going to pass through town for a brief visit on her way to an overseas assignment in India. This would be the last chance I'd have to see her for a very long time.

The circumstances were less than ideal. I was extremely fatigued from the radiation and a bit discouraged by the daily ordeal of having to visit the cold, sterile radiation lab. The atmosphere there was morbidly solemn; a sense of death lurked in every corner. Most of the people walking in and out of the place seemed stunned, not knowing whether they were going to live or die. The hospital personnel, who worked with dying people every day, were fairly desensitized, and whenever I arrived for my appointment they made minimal eye contact with me. The nurses focused strictly on the task at hand, dedicating themselves to keeping the patients on schedule and the medical interventions correct.

The night Connie arrived, I felt inspired. I'd had enough gloom and doom in that radiation lab. It was time to liven up the atmosphere and give those nurses a shot of good ol' down-to-earth fun. I concocted a plan and asked Connie if she would be my accomplice. Usually she would have jumped at the chance to pull a twin switch, but she was a bit uncomfortable doing it to professionals and people we really didn't know. Plus, being around radiation kind of scared her. But with a little cajoling on my part, she reluctantly agreed.

(Before I tell you any more, you need to know that early in my treatment the nurses had tattooed small dots on my chest where the radiation was to be administered. These marks are permanent. Okay, read on!)

While driving to the hospital the next morning, we asked God to please deposit some of His life and joy in that place of death. When we arrived, the nurses were busy with business behind the counter and didn't notice that two of us had entered instead of one. We went directly to the changing room, where I gave Connie my gown. Then I coached her on the procedure.

"After you change, go into the waiting area, and stay put until a nurse comes to get you. She'll take you to the radiation lab. When you get to the lab, climb up on the table, lie down, and raise your arm above your head."

Connie played along. I watched from inside the dressing room with the light off and the door slightly ajar. I wasn't about to miss seeing our scheme unfold.

A nurse arrived right on schedule and greeted Connie. "Good morning. How are you doing today?"

"Oh, it's been such a busy morning," Connie replied. "I'm feeling a little confused."

"Well, just follow me," the nurse said.

My sister hopped up on the table, lay down, and lifted her arm over her head per my instructions. But there was a problem. The next thing Connie heard was, "My goodness.

You *are* confused! Your head is at the wrong end of the table!"

Connie was so rattled by the obvious mistake that her hands began to tremble, making it hard for her to undo her gown for the next step in the treatment. The nurse was quick to pick up on it. "You're not only confused," she exclaimed. "You're nervous!"

Playing along, Connie said, "I just don't know what's wrong with me. I'm obviously not myself today."

Next the nurse needed to align the beams of light with the tattoos. But the marks were nowhere to be found. The nurse shrieked, "There are no tattoos!"

One of the other nurses, who had been working in the lab for more than five years, came running. "I've never seen anything like this before!" she exclaimed.

The two of them carefully searched for the dots. They paused only to look at each other with eyes the size of golf balls.

About that time I very nonchalantly walked out of the dressing room and asked the staff in a stern tone of voice, "What are you doing, giving radiation to the wrong patient?"

The technician almost fainted, and one of the nurses screamed, "There are two of you!" The rest of the staff erupted into such hilarious laughter that they could hardly catch their breath.

After the laughter subsided, I switched places with Connie and, sure enough, the dots were right where they had been the day before. I continued with treatment while Connie changed her clothes and took a seat in the waiting room.

A man who was waiting for his wife wanted to know what all the laughter in the other room was about, and Connie told him the story. Guffawing, he was almost falling out of his chair when his wife walked in. This piqued her curiosity, and she too wanted an explanation. When Connie told her what we had done, she doubled over in laughter. Then Connie noticed tears streaming down the husband's face. When he finally regained his composure, he hugged his wife tightly and said to Connie in a shaking voice, "Thank you. Thank you for doing this. My wife thinks she is dying, and this is the first time I've seen her laugh in three months."

The doctor administering my treatment turned to me and said, "You brought more healing today than any radiation ever could. Thank you for being brave enough to pull the switch—and for giving everyone a good, hard laugh!"

I love the twins' lighthearted spunk. It just goes to show you that a little levity can help blow your cares away.

Does something seem terribly important today? Are you distracted by anxieties that won't give you a moment of peace? Try to look for the funny side of life. And remember: Some things that seem terribly important and serious now might become absolutely hilarious after a little time passes.

Reclaim Your Life

FOOD FOR THOUGHT

So here's what I want you to do, God helping you:
Take your everyday, ordinary life—your sleeping, eating,
going-to-work, and walking-around life—and place it
before God as an offering.

ROMANS 12:1, THE MESSAGE

PRAYER FOR TODAY

Lord, why is it so hard to take care of myself? I act as if it's some great
flaw that I need rest and refreshment! The truth is that I am made in
Your image and made to need these things. I feel so overwhelmed right
now that the thought of worrying about anything else frightens me, but
I know I need to focus on the basics and on equipping myself to effec-
tively get through difficult or stressful times. Please, Lord, help me to
give myself some grace—to take a deep breath and realize that it's okay
to rest. And, while I take this breath, I want to actively remember all
Your loving ways and how You have provided for me in the past. Lord,
when I think of Your provision, I can do nothing but praise You. Thank
You for Your constant care. In Jesus' name, amen.

STEPS TO TAKE THIS MONTH

- Keep the basics in check. Are you sleeping? Exercising? Eating a balanced diet? Taking care of yourself isn't selfish; it's just smart. Focus on the basics this month.

- Make a list of all the times God has been faithful to you in the past and post it somewhere prominent (your bathroom mirror, the fridge, your desk). Read the list daily and add to it as you remember specific examples of God's goodness in your life.

- What small changes can you make today to reduce stimulation in your life? Turn off the news? Set the paper aside for a week? Seek out quiet time? Commit to these changes for one month and wait to see if peace follows and your worries diminish.

- Have you had a good laugh lately? Do yourself a favor and *let yourself laugh*. Set aside those anxieties and fears that are plaguing your day and find something to smile about.

ACKNOWLEDGE
YOUR ANGER

Anger is a legitimate response to certain situations.
It is not a bad emotion.

Chapter Sixteen

REMEMBER: IT'S
OKAY TO BE ANGRY

Go ahead and be angry. You do well to be angry—
but don't use your anger as fuel for revenge.

EPHESIANS 4:26, *THE MESSAGE*

or many years now my husband, John, has taught anger management classes. Some of those who attend his courses are there only because the court has required them to seek professional help. Others are average, get-up-and-go-to-work kinds of men and women who now and then lash out at their coworkers, spouses, or kids.

Whatever their backgrounds, they all have one pressing need: to learn to manage their anger constructively. John's goal is to give them the tools they need to do that.

John's students are not alone in their need to learn how to break destructive anger patterns. Research conducted during the 1990s showed that domestic violence was the number one reason women visited hospital emergency rooms. Focus on the Family, Dr. James Dobson's organization, surveyed children across America from all economic strata, asking them this question: If you could change one thing about your parents, what would it be? Ninety-six percent of the children said, "I wish they wouldn't get mad at me so much." Parents obviously struggle with anger. In fact, there isn't a person alive who doesn't find it difficult to handle anger now and then. And when anger is mismanaged, it can carry a very high cost.

One of the first things John does at the beginning of a class is to ask each person to complete this sentence: "I get angry when…" Over the years, the answers have been remarkably similar. Do any of these responses hit a nerve in you? If so, welcome to the human race. If not, please see your doctor to determine whether you have a pulse!

I GET ANGRY WHEN…

- I'm late and can't find my car keys.

- I make stupid mistakes.

- I know that someone isn't listening to me.

- I ask my kids to do something and they argue with me.

- I think someone is talking down to me.

- I feel controlled.

- I can't control things or make things work out.

- I'm the target of inconsiderate drivers.

- I feel threatened.

- I'm treated unfairly.

- I'm betrayed.

- I hear someone calling another person derogatory names.

- I feel that God doesn't answer my prayers.

- I see innocent people suffer.

Our responses to situations like these will differ depending on how much importance we attach to them. We aren't likely to get frustrated or angry about something that isn't important to us. The more it matters, the more intense our emotional responses. Anger can be viewed as part of a continuum:

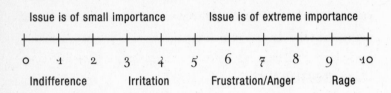

I'm sure that, with the exception of terrorists and their sympathizers, there were very few people who weren't angry in the aftermath of the terrorist attacks of September 11, 2001. In fact, in the face of this and other evil acts the absence of anger may indicate apathy, indifference, or a lack of compassion for others.

In his classes, John makes it clear that anger is a legitimate response to certain situations. "Our goal," he says, "is not to teach you how to stop being angry. We're starting this course with the assumption that anger is not a bad emotion. It's a normal, healthy emotion, and it's important that we acknowledge and feel it. And while it's a healthy emotion, it can also be a challenging one, as most of you already know.

"I'll say it again: The goal of this class isn't to help you stop feeling anger. When we try to deny or repress our feelings, we misspend our energies. Feelings that are stuffed don't go away; they just remain hidden. And when they remain hidden, they gain control over us. I've met some people who have hidden their feelings for so long that when they try to access them, they can't. They may not feel much anger, but they have no joy either.

"It's okay to be angry. But have you ever noticed how the word *anger* is one letter short of *danger*? The way we process and express our anger can be good, or it can be bad. The goal of this class is to help us learn how to be angry without blowing it. If we don't process our anger properly, we can create danger for ourselves and for others."

Anger is part of God's original design. In the Bible there are 450 references to God's anger, and because He created us in His image, we too have the capacity to be angry. Does this mean that God is an irritable tyrant? The only way we can answer that question is to examine the life of Jesus Christ, who fully revealed God's nature. There we see that God's anger is the result of His justice and His love and compassion for mankind.

Time and again in the Bible we read that Jesus was "moved with compassion." The Greek word for *compassion* literally means to experience a gut-wrenching sensation. His heart broke when He saw people in desperate need, unfairly oppressed, or grossly mistreated. A strong sense of empathy led Him to feed the hungry, heal the sick, comfort the mourning, and raise the dead. He grieved over the injustices He witnessed—and they made Him angry.

In Mark 3:1–5 we find the Pharisees condemning Jesus for healing a man on the Sabbath. According to their teaching, no work was allowed on the Sabbath, and they considered healing a form of work. The Scripture says that Jesus was "grieved for the hardness of their hearts" and that He "looked round about on them with anger" (v. 5, KJV).

Mark 10:13–16 tells us that Jesus became angry with His disciples when they tried to stop a group of children from approaching Him. He sternly rebuked the disciples, told them to let the children come to Him, and then laid His hands on the little ones and blessed them.

Perhaps the best-known example of Jesus' anger is found in Mark 11:15–17. Merchants and moneylenders had set up their businesses in the temple courts. Incensed, Jesus overturned their tables. "Is it not written, My house shall be called of all nations the house of prayer?" He cried. "But ye have made it a den of thieves" (v. 17, KJV).

Jesus was not indifferent to the sin and suffering in this world. In fact, it made Him angry, and His anger drove Him to take action on behalf of others, including laying down His own life so that the rest of us could be forgiven of our sins and thus receive eternal life. Jesus got angry, but He used His anger as God intended—for good.

Anger, properly channeled and controlled, is a good thing—a God-given thing. Sometimes our anger is an indication that we have a strong sense of justice, and people who become angry about injustice often make our world a better place to live.

Martin Luther's anger about the religious abuses of his time ushered in the Reformation. The Thirteenth Amendment was the fruit of agitation by abolitionists angry about the enslavement of human beings. Suffragists angry about their inability to vote initiated a campaign that resulted in the passage of the Nineteenth Amendment. Martin Luther King's anger about racism led to the Civil Rights Act of 1964.

All these people were angry, but they channeled their anger into positive action that brought about social reform. Certainly our national anger about terrorist attacks is a positive force that energizes the mission to bring the murderers to justice.

We all get angry, and it's okay to be angry.

Like a chainsaw, anger is not inherently destructive. It's a God-given emotion that has a function. But it can be helpful or harmful depending on how we use it. If we don't learn how to process and express it in healthy ways, the results can be ruinous.

To avoid these disasters and turn our anger toward good ends, we need to know what causes it and how we are likely to react when we feel angry. It's a vital component in letting go, and it's the subject of the next chapter.

Chapter Seventeen

RECOGNIZE YOUR ANGER STYLE

Everyone should be quick to listen, slow to speak
and slow to become angry, for man's anger does not bring
about the righteous life that God desires.

JAMES 1:19-20

*M*ost of us know what anger feels like, but do we know what it is? *Webster's New World Dictionary* defines it as "a hostile feeling of displeasure because of injury or opposition." Our response to this hostile feeling of displeasure has both biological and learned components.

Biologically speaking, anger is a survival reflex that we use instinctively when we're faced with some sort of threat. We know from medical research that when certain parts of the brain are electrically stimulated, it sends signals to the body to release chemicals into the bloodstream. In turn, these chemicals cause increased heart rate, shallow breathing, tense muscles, flushed skin, increased temperature, perspiration, and even shakiness. Our body goes on alert to protect us from harm and danger.

Dr. Theo Johnson, who has lectured on anger management for years, uses a clever acronym — RAT — for three basic perceptions that can trigger anger. It stands for Rejection, Attack, or Threat.[1] When we sense one of these, we "smell a rat." We feel anger, and our body prepares for action. Sometimes the energy that anger generates serves to protect us from physical danger.

When RATs are around, we instinctively get ready to fight or flee. At other times anger serves to protect us from psychological danger by preserving our dignity and self-esteem. The human body needs the mechanism of anger. If we didn't have it we wouldn't be able to protect ourselves—physically or psychologically.

Anger can also be a reaction to physical pain. Have you ever stubbed your toe on a piece of furniture and wanted to kick the table that got in your way? (Which only makes things worse!) Have you ever been physically hurt and instinctively wanted to hurt back? An automatic response like that once left John facing some rather embarrassing consequences. I'll let him tell you the story.

IN THE FALL OF 1974 I was a sophomore in college and in the middle of pre-season soccer practice. Our team was preparing for a season of intense competition, and we had high hopes of finishing first in our league. I was determined to give the team my very best.

During the first few weeks of practice, the coach divided the team into two sides and told us to scrimmage against each other. That was my favorite part of practice because it fueled my competitive fire. When the adrenaline kicked in, I focused every ounce of skill and determination to send the ball flying into the goal net.

When I got the ball, I sprinted down the field, dribbling and outmaneuvering the guys who tried to steal it. Making my way to center field, I saw my buddy Ted. That day he was playing on the opposing side, and there he was, running full speed at me. Seconds later we were waging war over the ball with our feet as each of us tried to dominate the other. Before I knew it, he kicked the ball full force into my groin. I reacted instantly by planting my fist on his mouth and knocking him to the ground. One of his teeth sliced my knuckle open, and we both ended up in the emergency room for stitches. I couldn't believe what I had done.

With an inquisitive grin on her face, the nurse cleaning my knuckle glanced over at Ted, who was sitting on a bed across the room. "I noticed that he came in the same time you did," she said. "Am I correct in assuming that your knuckle and his mouth had a head-on collision?"

I was too embarrassed to think that her comment was funny. "Yeah," I replied sheepishly.

She wasn't finished with her interrogation. "What school do you go to?" she asked, raising her eyebrows.

I hesitated. Covering my mouth with my good hand, I whispered, "Multnomah Bible College."

"I'm sorry," she said. "I didn't hear you."

I repeated myself a little louder.

She grinned again, and I expected her next question to be "So, is that how the school teaches you to handle conflict?" But she just said, "Ohhh."

When Ted and I finally made eye contact, I apologized for overreacting. He forgave me, and we both went back to campus.

The next day the dean called me into his office. The last time this sort of thing had happened to me was in seventh grade, when I was called into the principal's office after a playground squabble. Since then I had managed to steer clear of those kinds of situations, but now it was happening again, this time in the worst possible place—Bible college!

With my tail between my legs, I walked into the dean's office and sat down. Even though my actions had been in self defense, I was still in trouble.

Peering at me, the dean said, "John, I understand that you had a little run-in with one of the other students...and that you belted him in the mouth."

"Yes, sir," I said. "That's right."

"John, why did you come to Bible college?" he asked.

I wasn't sure where the conversation was going, but I told him that God had told me to quit my construction job and go to Bible college to prepare for the ministry. I saw a grin tugging at the corner of his mouth, but he quickly regained his composure and, with a very serious expression, said, "So you want to be a minister?"

"Yes, sir, I do...if God will still have me," I replied.

"Well, John," he said, "you might want to work on your anger and the way you react to others."

I laughed nervously, told him I agreed with him, and promised it would never happen again.

I made a concerted effort to keep that promise. Ted and I made amends, and neither of us held a grudge. It was a positive ending to a very embarrassing situation.

RATs can generate anger, and, as in John's case, so can physical pain. Whatever the stimulus, anger is an emotion that indicates that something is wrong and needs attention. Typically we learn to deal with it by observing those around us. During childhood we watch parents and siblings respond to situations and then mimic their behavior, trying our hand at influencing our environment and learning what works and what doesn't.

One of John's first recollections of an angry outburst was when he was about ten years old. He had been lying in bed, trying to go to sleep. His older sisters were still up, watching TV in the living room, laughing and talking very loudly. The noise was keeping him awake. He called out several times for them to be quiet, but they ignored him. Finally, when he couldn't take it anymore, he got out of bed and yelled at them. After that they were quiet. He learned that raising his voice got him what he wanted.

John's family outwardly expressed their emotions. They laughed loudly and talked passionately; they were exuberant over joys and emphatic about things that bothered them. As the third of five children, John witnessed the different anger styles of his older and younger siblings. Two of them tended to be compliant peacemakers who hid their anger. The other two were overtly aggressive. His parents also tended to be open with their conflicts and sometimes argued within hearing range of the children. Raised voices were common in his home.

My family modeled other ways of handling anger. As the oldest of three children, I didn't have any older siblings who stirred up conflicts with me. My brother and sister were four and six years behind me, so sibling rivalry really wasn't much of an issue. And I can't remember ever hearing my parents fight. That doesn't mean they didn't have their problems; it just means that we didn't know about them. They kept their conflicts private and tended to handle them quietly. They rarely raised their voices. As a result of this kind of home environment, I tend to hold in my feelings instead of letting them out. If I'm going to err in mismanaging my anger, it's going to be more internal than external. In the early years of our marriage I had to work very hard at not stuffing my anger.

In our counseling offices, John and I talk to many people who hide their anger because they think they are doing themselves and others a favor. But when we hold our anger in, hoping that it will just go away, we run the risk of creating other problems for ourselves. Stuffing anger doesn't get rid of it. It simply reroutes it. If bottled up, it will find an avenue of escape in our bodies. Psychosomatic disorders such as high blood pressure, headaches, lower-back pain, fatigue, and stomach problems can be the result of repressed anger.

Holding in our anger can injure our bodies, and it can also damage our relationships by keeping us from working through conflicts and getting beyond them. I recently met with a woman who described such an impasse:

> Jim called me from the airport and asked me to come pick
> him up. He had caught an earlier flight, which landed three
> hours ahead of his planned schedule. I was just walking out
> the door, as I had to drop off our son at basketball practice
> on my way to his parent-teacher conference. When I told
> Jim what I was in the process of doing, he said, "I'll catch
> a cab," and then hung up the phone. That was four days ago,
> and he still hasn't spoken to me! When I ask him what's
> wrong, he says in a curt tone of voice, "Nothing!"

The rerouting of Jim's anger didn't stop there. When his wife called the family to the dinner table, he went to his computer. When she packed him lunches to take to work, he left them in the refrigerator. In turn, she fed them to the dogs just to get back at him. In his anger, Jim stonewalled, and nothing got solved. Just the opposite occurred: The cold war between them intensified with each passing day. When Jim wasn't ranting, raving, or exploding, he was converting his anger into hostile acts that hurt the most important people in his life.

I remember hearing a story about Tommy Bolt, who is often described as the angriest golfer in the history of the game. He was giving a lesson to a group of golfers, teaching them how to hit a ball out of a sand trap. He called his eleven-year-old son over to him and said, "Show the people what your father has taught you to do when your shot lands in the sand." The young boy picked up a golf club and threw it as hard and as far as his little arm would let him. He had obviously learned his lessons well.

Some of us know that we have a problem with anger because it's too conspicuous for anyone to miss. We raise our voices, yell, turn red in the face, cry, curse, throw things, slam doors, or become violent or verbally abusive. Others disguise their anger so that it seems subtler and more socially acceptable. Dr. Willard Gaylan, professor of psychiatry at Columbia University's College of Physicians and Surgeons, wrote a book entitled *The Rage Within: Anger in Modern Life*. In it he says that some of the angriest people have learned to disguise their rage so well that they aren't even aware they're losing their temper.[2]

Even if we don't blow our lids or stuff our feelings, we might sulk, stew, or rehearse what we'd like to say to someone and brood about the one who "hurt" us. We might pull in, withdraw into self-pity or self-critical thoughts, give people the silent treatment, become more controlling, or withhold our love. Or we might use sarcasm and cutting humor, bad-mouth people behind their backs, and recruit people to side with us against others. An even more subtle form of anger is when we hear that something bad has happened to another and yet have no sympathy for them. We may, in fact, even feel a bit happy. This lack of empathy is an indication of anger.

If the way we express our anger is a learned behavior, the good news is that it can be unlearned. A new behavior can take its place. John and I wouldn't be counselors unless we were fully convinced that people can change. God doesn't play favorites. If He will help us with our anger problems, He will help you.

A good way to start is by recognizing our anger styles. After that, we need to ask a very important question: Do circumstances and other people make us angry, or do we make ourselves angry? We'll answer that question in the next chapter.

Reclaim Your Life

FOOD FOR THOUGHT

> *Hot tempers start fights;*
> *a calm, cool spirit keeps the peace.*

PROVERBS 15:18, *THE MESSAGE*

Anger is part of God's original design.

PRAYER FOR TODAY

Father in heaven, I feel angry about certain things. Sometimes I stuff these feelings because they seem wrong, and at other times I explode. Neither of these reactions seems to be working. Lord, please help me to acknowledge and process my anger properly. In those moments when I'm about to blow, please remind me of the way You handled Your anger. Please help me to learn to express my anger properly, in the way that would please You most. In Jesus' name I pray, amen.

STEPS TO TAKE THIS MONTH

- *Angry?* God has given us permission to be angry, so go ahead and let yourself feel that emotion. Don't stuff the anger; acknowledge your emotion.

- And now let's think about processing it properly. What are some examples from your past of times when you haven't handled your anger properly? What could you have done differently?

- Have you identified your anger style? What is it?

- How does your anger style differ from those close to you? Your spouse? Family members? Coworkers? What can you do to make interactions during stressful times go more smoothly?

RESOLVE YOUR ANGER

*If we want to let go of our anger,
we must quit playing judge and jury
and accept the limits and imperfections
we see in ourselves and others.*

Chapter Eighteen

RECITE THE ABCS OF ANGER

If you are pained by an external thing, it is not this thing that disturbs you—but your judgment about it.

MARCUS AURELIUS

Have you ever heard people make statements like these?

"He makes me so mad!"

"She infuriates me!"

"My kids are driving me crazy!"

"If it weren't for so and so, I wouldn't have blown my cool!"

Have you ever said something similar? If we're honest, most of us have to admit that we occasionally point to someone else as the cause of our anger.

There's only one problem with that idea: It doesn't help. Not one bit.

We can't control our anger as long as we believe that others cause it. We have to take responsibility for fueling the fires that rage within, as well as for dousing them. As long as we believe that the cause of our anger is outside ourselves, we will never be able to master it.

John has a favorite line that he asks his class members to repeat throughout his course: "The truth is: I make me mad." He drives the point home by regularly reiterating: "My wife doesn't make me mad.

138

My kids don't make me mad. My boss doesn't make me mad. My coworkers don't make me mad. The guy who cuts me off on the freeway doesn't make me mad. *I make me mad!*"

People, as well as situations and events, can trigger our thoughts and beliefs about something, which can in turn make us angry. But in most cases they do not cause our anger. It's what we think and tell ourselves about that person, situation, or event that fuels it.

Dr. Albert Ellis, a pioneer of cognitive behavioral therapy, contends that "crooked thinking" plays a key part in creating emotional conflicts. He says that it's important to look at the ABCs of anger—the events and thoughts that precede the emotion—because the more we understand the irrational things we say to ourselves when we're angry, the better we'll be able to properly process and control our feelings.[4] John and I have found the ABC tool powerful and effective in helping people who are troubled by their anger.

We are what we think. And what we think leads to feelings. Some thoughts make us happy; some make us sad. Others make us angry. The beauty of the ABC tool is that it underscores the fact that we can change our emotional responses to situations by changing what we tell ourselves. This gives us an enormous amount of control over what we feel and do. Let's look at it in detail and trace the chain reaction that leads to anger.

A stands for the *activating* event, or the assumed cause of our anger. This could be any number of things: getting a flat tire on the way to work, not getting the promotion you wanted, a sales clerk hovering when you want to be left alone, someone you've made plans with backing out at the last minute, or your children doing precisely what you've asked them not to.

An activating event can also be a thought about the past or the future that concerns you. For example, when I remember the moment we received word from the doctor that our son Nathan had been born with Down's syndrome, that memory serves as an activating event. It triggers thoughts that in turn trigger feelings. The *external* activating event triggers our *internal* thoughts and beliefs.

B stands for our *beliefs* and the things that we tell ourselves about the activating events. Some of our beliefs are rational. They help us cope, manage, adjust, and turn down the heat. Other beliefs are irrational, or "crooked." They are not helpful and can actually perpetuate our distress.

C stands for the *consequences* that result from our beliefs and what we say to ourselves. Our internal dialogue evokes a wide array of emotions, one of which can be anger. The various ways we express our anger through our behavior can also be viewed as consequences.

I recently talked with Larry and Karen, who have been married a little over two years. Both are young, full-time graduate school students deeply devoted to their respective fields of study. Wanting to maintain a strong marriage, they had set aside Wednesday night as date night, a time to just be alone together and have fun. But when it was time to register for classes for the second semester of the school year, Larry signed up for one held on Monday and Wednesday nights from 6:00 to 9:00 p.m.

When Karen heard about it she was livid—so angry that she didn't speak to him for two days. She believed that her anger was due to the fact that Larry had reneged on his commitment to their date night. In other words, she believed that *A*, the activating event (Larry's schedule change), caused *C*, the consequence (her anger and silent withdrawal).

I introduced the ABC tool into the counseling session and asked Karen to think about the *B* in the equation. Bright and insightful, she easily identified what she believed about Larry's schedule change:

His classes are more important than I am.

He doesn't care about our marriage as much as he used to. Our date night must not matter to him.

If he bails on this, what else is he going to bail on?

These beliefs fueled Karen's anger. She thought they were true. When she and Larry entered my office, I could feel the wall of ice between them. As the counseling session progressed and both expressed their views, it became evident that Karen was caught in the trap of crooked thinking. But once she heard the rationale behind Larry's actions, her beliefs changed and her anger subsided.

Larry made it clear to Karen that date nights were a top priority and that he had planned to talk with her about switching "their" night to Friday, since she didn't have any other commitments that night. Friday was the night he usually shot hoops with a couple of friends down at the local gym, but he was planning to give that up in order to be with her. Karen also learned that the class Larry had signed up for was a required course that was offered only once a year. If he didn't take the class that semester, he wouldn't graduate when he expected to. With this new information, Karen's beliefs changed. Now she believed:

Larry does care about our marriage.

Our date nights do matter to him.

He never intended to bail on me.

His willingness to give up basketball on Fridays shows how much he loves me.

As a result of her new beliefs, Karen's feelings toward Larry went from cold and guarded to warm and fuzzy.

The facts of the situation had not determined how Karen felt; her perception of the facts had evoked the negative emotion. Her beliefs about Larry's choices turned out to be quite different from the actual reasons for them. Once she gave him a chance to share his thoughts with her, she realized that her assumptions were faulty. When the new beliefs replaced the old beliefs, the anger went away.

The important thing to remember about the ABCs is that we don't get from *A* to *C* without going through *B*. Understanding the nature of our beliefs—knowing whether they are rational or irrational—is a big part of properly processing our anger. Anger doesn't have to be an overpowering or unmanageable part of our personalities. As we change our thinking, we can change our emotions.

In his extensive years of research and clinical practice, Dr. Ellis identified several distorted beliefs that are commonly held by emotionally disturbed people. If you hang on to any of these twisted beliefs, you will most likely struggle with frequent and intense feelings of anger:

- I must be liked or loved by everyone.

- I must be an expert at everything in order to be worthwhile.

- I have no control over my own happiness. My feelings are caused by what happens to me.

- It's easier to avoid life's difficulties and responsibilities than it is to face them.

- It's absolutely awful if things don't turn out the way I want them to.

- There's a right and perfect solution to all problems, and it's bad if I can't find it.

- I must experience pleasure rather than pain.

- If people don't treat me fairly, they are wicked and deserve punishment.

As you can see, these unrealistic expectations can easily ignite anger. There is no possible way that everyone will like us or that we can be experts at everything we do. Human beings are fallible creatures who exist in imperfect societies, which often don't function according to fair rules. We set ourselves up for anger and emotional disturbances when we convince ourselves that we have a right to expect these things. If these crooked beliefs are rooted in our minds, we will not experience peace and contentment. However, when we realize that they are absurd and replace them with rational thoughts, we can turn down the heat of the fires that rage within.

Did you notice how many musts there are in crooked thinking? We want to be on the lookout for any thoughts that include an absolute, such as *must, should, ought,* or *have to.* Thoughts like *I must...* or *You should...* or *They ought to...* put intense pressure on us, on others, and on the situations we're facing. They trigger frustration and anger.

We can easily upset others and ourselves by thinking that things have to be exactly the way we want them to be. An irritated mother fumes, *My kids must clean up their rooms this minute!* A frustrated businessman insists, *I have to get this order nailed down by this afternoon.* An angry driver thinks, *The guy in front of me should either learn how to drive or get off the road!* An unhappy college student repeatedly tells herself, *I have to pledge that sorority in order to be happy.* A young woman in a bad situation prays over and over, *God, You should have stopped this from happening to me.* Thoughts fraught with oughts and shoulds energize anger. The more we turn up the demands, the more we fan our emotional flames.

Besides erasing the musts, shoulds, and oughts from our internal dialogue, it's also important to avoid thoughts that in one way or another say, *This is so terrible that I can't stand it!* A comment like this simply generates more anger and makes us less effective in problem solving. A more rational way to think about our distress is to tell ourselves, *I don't like this situation or feeling angry, but I can tolerate it. I can manage to live a good life in spite of this frustration. God promises to give me the strength to endure whatever comes my way. He also promises to give me the wisdom I need to straighten out my crooked thinking.*

With God's help and some time and effort in these areas, we will gain skill in processing our thoughts, and we will let our anger go.

Chapter Nineteen

REMAIN CALM

A fool gives full vent to his anger,
but a wise man keeps himself under control.

PROVERBS 29:11

We've just looked at the ABC tool for working through anger. You may think you're in the middle of an alphabet soup at this point, but I have one more three-letter tool for your tool bag.

Ready? It's PPP.

This is a wonderful acronym. And, if you use it, I have a promise for you: It will help you for the rest of your life! PPP stands for three steps: *Pause! Ponder! Pray!*

PAUSE

The first step is to deliberately pause—to decrease the arousal and buy yourself some time. Allow your body and emotions to cool down before you take action. You may even want to physically leave the situation you're in. If you don't, things can quickly go from bad to worse.

Have you ever noticed that the angrier we get, the dumber we get? When we're angry, the greatest favor we can do for others and ourselves is to pause. Call a time out, knowing you will come back to the issue later. The pause is not a maneuver to punish, reject, hurt, or abandon those with whom we are upset. It's simply used to buy us some time to calm down.

When you're in *pause* mode, take several deep, cleansing breaths and deliberately relax whatever muscles are tense. Walk around the room, shake out the tension, or lean back in your chair in a relaxed posture. Roll your shoulders and neck. Get a drink of water. Take a power walk, if you can, to push the tension out of your body. Do whatever you need to do to pull your body out of agitation.

PONDER

Ask yourself, *What is driving my anger? What do I want that I'm not getting?* Self-awareness is an important key to managing anger. Evaluate what is bugging you so you can turn down the heat on your anger. Take a look at what you are saying to yourself. Are your words turning up the heat or calming you down?

Think cool! Try to use cool words when you're mad at someone. Here's a sample: "Getting angry won't get me what I want in the long run. Think straight. Keep focused. Stay positive. Keep reason and respect number one. Don't blame; look for solutions. Try to understand the other person's point of view. This situation isn't worth a coronary. This problem is annoying, but I don't have to let it become a big deal. Lighten up. You don't have to take this so seriously. God will help me find a solution. Conflict is a part of life. I can handle this."

PRAY

When we tell God about our hurt and anger, we do so for our sake, not His. He already knows the secrets of our hearts anyway. When I say "pray," I'm not talking about fancy, pious, religious words. I'm talking about simple, authentic thoughts and feelings about what is bugging us, like what Kim does in the following story.

For sixteen years after I completed my MBA at Harvard, I was the only woman among the eight vice presidents of a successful corporation. I believed that God had opened the door for me to be there and that He had given me the education and experience I needed to succeed. I loved my job and the people I worked with, and I planned to stay with the firm until I retired.

One afternoon the CEO called me into his office. He spoke enthusiastically about my bright future with the corporation and told me that he saw bigger and better things ahead for me. As I listened I became very excited about the new opportunities for growth and service that seemed to be opening up for me. Although he didn't go into detail about what my new job would be, he asked me to prepare for it by training two of the people I supervised so they could assume my current responsibilities.

When I finished training them six weeks later, the CEO again called me in for a meeting. Since I was expecting him to talk about my new duties, I was stunned when he told me that my position had been eliminated.

"It's nothing personal," he said. "It's just that we've terminated the position. But there's another in-house position that's open, and you're welcome to that."

That job paid half of what I made as a vice president and required me to report to a man in his twenties who had just graduated from college. Although I was barely able to comprehend what was happening, one thing was clear: The CEO wanted to get rid of me. I resigned, and for months afterward my anger burned at my boss for his betrayal.

I couldn't sleep. Thoughts of the way he had treated me invaded my dreams or kept me awake heaving huge sighs of frustration. I pictured him losing his job in a hostile takeover or being publicly exposed. The longer I held on to my anger, the fewer good things I could find to say about him. My anger was so deep and pervasive that I was becoming the exact opposite of the person I wanted to be. It was also hurting me much more than it was my boss, and I knew that I had to find a way to let it go and get on with my life. But how?

One thing was clear: I couldn't do it alone. I needed God's help, and I began to talk to Him about my feelings day and night. As angry as I was, listening to what He was saying to me was more difficult, but, even so, it soon became clear to me that He was prompting me to do a few things.

When I found myself obsessed with memories of the injustice, I pictured myself writing down all the events on a huge blackboard. Then, after I recorded all of the things that my mind wouldn't let go of, I picked up a big eraser, wiped the board clean, and told God that I couldn't carry these thoughts around in my head any longer. They were His to handle now, not mine.

I don't typically keep a journal, but during that difficult time I somehow felt the need to register my concerns with God in a concrete way. At first I felt embarrassed to write about my hurt and anger because it seemed like I was whining, but after journaling for a while I began to feel emotional relief. It also brought clarity by giving me added perspective. After a time I could reread what I'd written earlier and realize that I didn't feel quite as angry anymore.

The more I journaled, the more I found myself recording insights from Scripture that seemed to apply directly to my situation. When I came across a verse that spoke to my circumstances, I saw it as a promise from God, and I tried my best to *act* like I believed it. That helped me to focus on God and today instead of on my boss and the past. One of the verses that helped me the most was: "God is not unjust; he will not forget your work and the love you have shown him as you have helped his people and continue to help them" (Hebrews 6:10).

That verse gave me the confidence I needed to start over. I knew that I wanted to continue to help people and to love them as I had the people I'd worked with for so many years. So, after giving myself time to weigh the alternatives, I decided to become a freelance consultant. Committing myself to this new venture was another big step in the healing process.

Even so, it took almost a year for my anger to completely subside. And that doesn't mean I don't still feel the pain of the wound now and then, because I do. But the anger doesn't control me. Obsessing over the wrong doesn't dominate my thoughts or rule my life. As I look back now, I can see that when I took my turmoil to God in prayer, He was faithful to help me by showing me some specific and creative ways to let my anger go.

In the midst of the pain and confusion that accompany situations in which we struggle with anger, we need to pause, ponder, and pray. We need to turn to God and say, *God, I need Your help. Give me Your perspective. Let my eyes see as You see. Let my heart hear Your heart. Grant me insight into what You are doing in my life right now. Show me what I need to do to cooperate with You in letting my anger go.* And then we need to pay very close attention to the whisperings of the Holy Spirit and be mindful of the insights that bubble to the surface—because God will be faithful to answer those kinds of prayers.

Chapter Twenty

RESIST THE PHARISEE SYNDROME

*And do not bring sorrow to God's Holy Spirit by the way
you live.... Get rid of all bitterness, rage, anger, harsh words,
and slander, as well as all types of malicious behavior.*

EPHESIANS 4:30-31, NLT

I was angry.

John and I had had an argument the night before, and I was having a hard time letting go of the ill feelings it had triggered.

Yes, it was a petty thing. Aren't most fights about petty things?

We had been scheduled to shoot a video series for married couples on a particular date. John was certain he had told me the date, but I was sure he hadn't. I had told him that an out-of-town guest was coming that weekend, and he had entered his reminder on another weekend. So now we had to reschedule the video shoot, which was embarrassing for us and an inconvenience to the people involved.

Neither of us was happy with the other. Someone could have parked a truck in the middle of our king-size bed that night, and we never would have known it. We were both hugging the edges.

Silly, isn't it? Two educated adults who teach couples how to achieve intimacy in their marriages end up in a standoff about a scheduling mix-up. Oh, we both had our rational arguments.

But I didn't want to hear his, and he didn't want to hear mine. And make no mistake: This time, I wanted him to be the first to say he was sorry. As far as I was concerned, he had made the bigger error.

The Pharisee within me stood tall, refusing to budge an inch.

And the results? Anger. Alienation from my partner in life. Self-deception. And grief to the Spirit of God. That's the power of the Pharisee syndrome. It leads us to believe that we are faultless—or at least less at fault than another—that we know better, that we *are* better. Linked tightly with pride, it's a spiritual disease that drives anger and destroys relationships.

I went back and reread the parable of the Pharisee:

{Jesus} told his next story to some who were complacently pleased with themselves over their moral performance and looked down their noses at the common people: "Two men went up to the Temple to pray, one a Pharisee, the other a tax man. The Pharisee posed and prayed like this: 'Oh, God, I thank you that I am not like other people—robbers, crooks, adulterers, or, heaven forbid, like this tax man. I fast twice a week and tithe on all my income.'

"Meanwhile the tax man, slumped in the shadows, his face in his hands, not daring to look up, said, 'God, give mercy. Forgive me, a sinner.'"

Jesus commented, "This tax man, not the other, went home made right with God. If you walk around with your nose in the air, you're going to end up flat on your face, but if you're content to be simply yourself, you will become more than yourself." (Luke 18:9–14, *The Message*)

I sighed and turned to my Father in heaven: *Well, I guess that about hits the nail on the head, Lord. That's how I feel today—like someone who is flat on my face, without much oomph to get up. Okay, I get the message; I forgive John.*

By the way, my feelings were saying the exact opposite, but I knew I needed to choose to let go of my anger anyway. I knew that if I didn't respond to what God was showing me, things were not going to get better within me or in my relationship with John. I sensed the Holy Spirit's sadness over the hardness of our hearts toward each other. God is love, and anything that isn't love pains Him. A thought crossed my mind: *It is more important to love than to be right.*

So I prayed some more. *Lord, please forgive me for acting like a Pharisee. I detest how I think and act when I play that role. I don't want to be a person who is stubborn, self-willed, and critical. I surrender my need to be right to You and ask You to help John and me make things right between us.*

Then I called John at work and apologized for my part in the conflict. He apologized for his. It wasn't a conversation for a Hallmark commercial. No warm fuzzies were present for either of us. And when I hung up the phone I was amazed at how unrelenting the Pharisee within me was to make a point. I was still secretly hoping that John had grasped the fact that I was right and he was wrong. My, oh my, pride dies hard!

I'm so glad that God is bigger than my dark side. I'm so thankful that I'm not alone in my struggle. I think of the candid words Paul spoke to the Romans about his own battles:

I truly delight in God's commands, but it's pretty obvious that not all of me joins in that delight. Parts of me covertly rebel, and just when I least expect it, they take charge.

I've tried everything and nothing helps. I'm at the end of my rope. Is there no one who can do anything for me? Isn't that the real question? (Romans 7:22–24, *The Message*)

And I find hope in how he responds to the question raised:

The answer, thank God, is that Jesus Christ can and does. He acted to set things right in this life of contradictions where I want to serve God with all my heart and mind, but am pulled by the influence of sin to do something totally different.... God's Spirit is right alongside helping us along. (Romans 7:25; 8:26, *The Message*)

Just in case you're wondering, the rest of the day wasn't exactly fabulous, but it was a whole lot better. We gave up our attempts to persuade each other and made efforts to repair the breach. John realized that he had overreacted, and I realized that I had overreacted to his overreaction. It wasn't a fairy-tale ending, but at least we were on the same page! When we went to sleep that night, the anger and the space in the middle of the bed were gone. And so was the Holy Spirit's grief.

I wish I could say that it's easy for me to let go of anger. And I wish I could say that I always trust God—that I never argue, talk back, or demand my own way. But I can't, because at times I find myself doing those very things.

I remember one night when I was rocking Nathan to sleep. My soul was as dark as the night. Nathan was approaching a birthday, and birthdays seem to trigger both joy and grief, even when I try to focus on celebration. We have so much for which to be thankful. But on that particular night I must have been especially worn out, because my "attitude of gratitude" had flown the coop. I was in the middle of a power struggle with God.

I didn't want Nathan to be mentally retarded. I wanted him to be "normal."

I didn't want Nathan to be mute. I longed to hear his thoughts and feelings.

I didn't want Nathan to need special assistance at school and church. I wanted Nathan to be independent and capable like Jessie and Ben.

Looking back, I think I honestly believed that I knew what was best for Nathan and the rest of us, and it didn't include a diagnosis of Down's syndrome. The Pharisee in me declared, "I want what I want when I want it!" And I was angry because I hadn't gotten my way.

I had been in this place before, struggling with the discrepancy between the ideal and the real. *How*, I wondered, *am I going to plan a fun-filled birthday party for Nathan while I'm in the middle of throwing myself a first-class pity party?* Tears fell, and I rocked Nathan for a long time that evening—more for my sake than his.

During those quiet moments an unexpected insight came to me. I sensed God saying, *Pam, I always give you My best.* The truth penetrated the core of my soul, and I wept. God had shone a spotlight on my prideful, stubborn will, and I realized that my resistance to the fact that Nathan was handicapped was the cause of much of my anguish.

Have you ever noticed that resisting circumstances does not change things? What is, is. Wrestling with reality gets us nowhere...except angry. But we can trust that no matter where we are at a particular time in our lives, God wants to give us His best. Resisting the Pharisee syndrome and letting God be God is the first step to accepting our circumstances and letting go of our anger.

For all of us, whatever our circumstances, the realization that "this is not what I want" triggers anger. But we don't always get what we want, and admitting that presents us with a choice. We can act like petulant children. We can argue, resist, slam doors, demand our way, and pout. Or we can surrender to the Lord our God and focus on the truth that He has a good plan for our lives and that His intention is to bless us. We can clench our fists and shake them in angry defiance, or we can open our hands in acceptance and ask God to take what we yield to Him and give us His best.

A passage in the book of Jeremiah can help us put things in perspective:

> The LORD gave another message to Jeremiah. He said, "Go down to the shop where clay pots and jars are made. I will speak to you while you are there." So I did as he told me and found the potter working at his wheel. But the jar he was making did not turn out as he had hoped, so the potter squashed the jar into a lump of clay and started again.
> Then the LORD gave me this message: "O Israel, can I not do to you as this potter has done to his clay? As the clay is in the potter's hand, so are you in my hand." (18:4-6, NLT)

Hard things happen in this world. No one warned us that this particular phase of the journey would be this dark. Yet as we dwell in the Potter's hands, even though we may be confused, in pain, and angry, we can trust that God is at work shaping us. For what? For what Paul called His "noble purposes." In pure faith we can rest, knowing that His intentions are good and that His direction is strategic. He is transforming us into His image. He's removing impurities and refining us like gold. It's our job to be pliable in His strong and tender hands.

We can trust that God cares about what we hold dear to our hearts. In time, more clarity will come. He really can make all things work together for our best—even the strange, unplanned situations that blindside us and tempt us to lash out in anger. We can trust that in the years ahead we will look back on today's painful circumstances and see how God used them to shape us into vessels worthy of honor. Even our worst mistakes can become springboards that launch us into divine assignments.

That dark night as I sat rocking Nathan, my divine assignment was to make a holy exchange: my anger, pride, and pharisaical demands for God's assurance that the Potter was at work. I needed to become less childish and more childlike—like Nathan, relaxed, sleeping soundly in my arms, confident that all was well.

It's all about letting go.

Chapter Twenty-One

RESOLVE UNMET NEEDS

And my God will meet all your needs
according to his glorious riches in Christ Jesus.

PHILIPPIANS 4:19

athy, whose husband, Matt, was counseling with John, re-
quested an appointment with me to discuss some things that
were troubling her. This couple had a daughter who was born with
Down's syndrome, and I thought Cathy might want to focus on issues
pertaining to her. My assumption was wrong: She was so angry with
Matt that she was entertaining the idea of divorce.

At first glance, Cathy seemed to have a great life. Matt was a
very successful businessman who provided her with many luxuries,
including a big home in a lovely part of town. She enjoyed living in
beautiful surroundings, and his substantial income allowed her to
decorate their home as she wanted.

Cathy had always wanted to be a stay-at-home mom, and Matt
fully supported her desire. Their son was a well-adjusted youngster,
a good student, and an athlete. Despite her handicap, their daughter functioned very well and was in good health. Although Matt was
on the job fifty hours a week, he was with the family most evenings
and weekends and was actively involved in the children's lives.

Matt was fulfilling many of Cathy's desires, but she was still angry and unhappy. She told me that Matt did not meet her emotional needs and that she longed for a soul mate who would share intimate thoughts and feelings with her.

As Cathy described the man of her dreams, it seemed to me that her ideal lover came straight from the pages of a Harlequin romance. In fact, I later learned that one of her favorite pastimes was reading romance novels. As I listened to her it occurred to me that her romantic expectations of marriage would never be met, because what she longed for was an unrealistic fantasy fed by Hollywood fairy tales and softcover fiction. The more she nurtured the fantasy, the angrier and more dissatisfied she was with Matt for not meeting her needs.

Cathy is not alone. Harlequin Publishers sells hundreds of millions of paperbacks a year. I've had women in therapy tell me that they were hooked on romance novels much like a cocaine addict is hooked on the drug. Now, don't get me wrong: I'm all for curling up with a good book as a diversion from the stresses of life. But a persistent diet of romance novels can stir up unrealistic expectations in marriage and leave women feeling as though their husbands have shortchanged them.

"Cathy, I'd like to ask you a question," I said. "May I?" She nodded her head, giving me the go-ahead.

"Cathy, you have an eight-year-old daughter with Down's syndrome. Do you expect your daughter to be able to do what your son did when he was eight years old?"

"Of course not!" she replied. "She's handicapped. There's no way!"

"So, are you saying that you've adjusted your expectations of her because she's handicapped?" I inquired.

"Well, sure." she said. "It would be silly not to."

After asking her permission to speak frankly, I said, "It's just about as silly to expect your husband to meet all your emotional needs. There's no way he can. He has some handicaps, just like the rest of the men on this planet. They're not taught how to meet the emotional needs of a woman. They spend much of their emotional energy providing for their families. And when you think about it, women are just as handicapped in their abilities to meet all the needs of a man."

I don't think I told Cathy what she wanted to hear that day, but she thanked me for the time we had together and said she'd think things through. A couple of weeks later she came back to my office toting the book *Men Are From Mars, Women Are From Venus*. She said she wanted to learn more about the differences between men and women. It was a sign to me that she was open to reconsidering her expectations of Matt.

As time passed, Cathy worked on defining her most important needs and communicating them more clearly to Matt. She realized that her way of asking him for closeness was too vague and that it usually ended up sounding like a complaint. Rather than commenting on his lack of attentiveness, she started suggesting that they do some things together that she enjoyed. She also took the initiative to plan quarterly weekend getaways for them so they could focus on each other without all the typical interruptions at home.

Matt wanted the marriage to work, and as he continued his counseling with John, he learned how to be more tuned in and responsive to the things that mattered to Cathy. Having grown up without a father in his home, Matt had to learn these skills in his thirties. In all honesty, he didn't become a flaming romantic, but he did grow in his ability to express thoughtfulness and affection.

One of the most fulfilling choices Cathy made was to start attending a women's group at their church. The new friendships she made there took the pressure off Matt to be the only person meeting her relational needs. Hearing the challenges other women faced in marriage also opened her eyes to Matt's many strengths. Cathy learned to not let her fantasies fuel her expectations of Matt, to be thankful for the needs he was able to meet, and to let go of the anger she had held on to for years.

I want to mention a related fact: Many men who seek counseling for help with anger speak of having, or having had, a problem with pornography or other sexual addictions. One man who attended John's anger management class as well as a recovery group for sexual addiction told John that his feelings of anger were as good at covering up his inner conflicts as pornography was. Both created a sort of high that effectively numbed his feelings of loneliness and inadequacy.

That is not surprising, because the chemical release that occurs in the brain in response to sexual stimulation and anger is similar. There is an addictive element to this chemical release because eventually the high of the past no longer satisfies, and a person has to increase the activity to get the same kind of fix.

In *Pure Desire*, Dr. Ted Roberts points out the potential consequences of this kind of addiction:

Sexual activity and fantasy, which produce the sense of pleasure, can actually alter a person's brain chemistry. This altered brain chemistry is a beautiful experience between a husband and wife. But when it is taken out of this context, it is the "high," not the relationship that becomes the focus. The other person is not important because he or she is simply the object that delivers the fix. This is why a sex addict can pursue seemingly irrational courses of action, such as repeated relationships with women other than his wife, or even prostitutes, despite the fact that he declares that he loves God. He gets a "buzz" from the danger of it.[4]

Intense anger not only gives a similar sort of buzz but also fuels marital infidelity. In all the years John and I have been counselors, we haven't met anyone who was unfaithful to his or her spouse who didn't have a problem with anger. Sometimes the anger was obvious, but not always. We've met many people in the midst of affairs who were experts at camouflaging their anger or driving it underground. Making choices against your conscience and your personal convictions takes an emotional push, and the emotion that energizes that push is anger.

I say all of this simply to underline the fact that fantasies, anger, sexual addictions, and infidelity are connected. We often find these issues mentioned together in Scripture. In a letter to the Corinthian church, the apostle Paul says:

I am afraid that when I come...there may be quarreling, jealousy, outbursts of anger, factions, slander, gossip, arrogance and disorder...and I will be grieved over many who have sinned earlier and have not repented of the impurity, sexual sin and debauchery in which they have indulged. (2 Corinthians 12:20–21)

And in a letter to the church at Colosse he says this:

Put to death...whatever belongs to your earthly nature: sexual immorality, impurity, lust.... You used to walk in these ways, in the life you once lived. But now you must rid yourselves of all such things as these: anger, rage, malice, slander, and filthy language from your lips. (Colossians 3:5, 7–8)

Sexual immorality and anger are joined at the hip. Often the anger stems from unmet needs either within the marriage or within other significant relationships, past or present. When people allow such needs to continue unattended, they become vulnerable to rationalizing their behavior in a way that allows them to seek instant gratification. Unhealthy choices are driven by angry beliefs like *If so-and-so won't give me what I want, then I'll get it another way, and I don't care if I have to break a few rules to do it.*

Resolving unmet needs can diffuse anger and diminish the likelihood of making other unhealthy choices. Sometimes we can meet these needs by making changes on the outside or within our environments. Other times we can satisfy them by making changes on the inside, such as revising our expectations. Still, I don't know anyone who feels that all of his or her needs are met all of the time. There are times when this just isn't possible, particularly if the changes we desire involve another person. Like it or not, we cannot force others to change.

The complete fulfillment of our physical, psychological, and spiritual needs will be realized only in heaven. Until then, we will all have some unmet needs, and we need God to help us sort through these challenges. He alone knows when we suffer in silence, confused and conflicted about the empty spaces in our souls. He knows what we're missing. He takes stock of our insufficiencies, and He promises to meet our needs as no one else can.

Henri Nouwen reminded me of this in his book *The Road to Daybreak*. A Catholic priest trained at Yale University, Nouwen held a professorship at Harvard and traveled the world as a renowned author and lecturer. Midway through his career, he left behind prestige and power to serve severely handicapped people in France. In his book he chronicles his spiritual journey during those years of transition, and in this journal entry he makes it clear that God alone can meet our deepest needs:

> It is hard for me to speak of my feelings of being rejected or imposed upon, of my desire for affirmation as well as my need for space, of insecurity and mistrust, of fear and love. But as I entered into these feelings, I also discovered the real problem—expecting from a friend what only Christ can give....
> I learned afresh that friendship requires a constant willingness to forgive each other for not being Christ, and a willingness to ask Christ himself to be the true center. When Christ does not mediate a relationship, that relationship easily becomes demanding, manipulating, oppressive, an arena for many forms of rejection. An unmediated friendship cannot last long; you simply expect too much of the other and cannot offer the other the space he or she needs to grow.[2]

Our family and friends can meet some of our needs, but ultimately God is the one who is all-sufficient. He has given us His Word. He has promised to give us wisdom. He will enable us to examine our unmet needs, revise unrealistic expectations, and let our anger go.

We have only to ask.

Chapter Twenty-Two

RELINQUISH CONTROL

The greatness of a man's power is the measure of his surrender.

WILLIAM BOOTH

I just don't get it!" Bob exclaimed. "When my boss gives me an assignment, I find myself eager to work long hours and do a top-notch job. But if he gives me a task and then goes on and on about every little detail involved, I start feeling resistant—like I want to tune him out." Confused by his conflicting feelings, Bob had come to John for help.

"When your boss is giving you a long list of instructions, do you feel angry?" John asked.

"I don't know if it's anger or not," Bob replied. "It just feels as though he's trying to micromanage my job."

"Sounds like you don't like feeling micromanaged," John observed.

"You've got that right! I was hired to do a job, and I wish he'd just let me do it. He has this thing about everything having to be done his way. But what about my own creativity? I have some great things to offer his business if he'd just give me some breathing room."

John probed further. "Bob, can you remember times in your past when you felt like this?"

"Oh, sure—when I was a kid. There was a lot of tension in my house. My dad was an army man. His word was law. We were all expected to obey him, no questions asked. I could never talk frankly about things that bothered me. If I had a complaint, Dad told me not to be a wimp and then shut me out. I remember when I wanted to take computer classes in junior high. He laughed it off and said that kind of stuff was for sissies. He wanted to control everything I did. There were times when I wanted to deck the guy."

Bob took a deep breath, sighed in distress, and looked at the floor.

"It sounds as if your anger was simply a cry of protest against a very rigid environment," John remarked. "Does your anger with your boss seem similar to the anger you felt with your father?"

Bob paused for a moment to think and then replied, "Yes, I suppose it does."

Perhaps you grew up in a rigid environment similar to Bob's, where you lived under a set of dogmatic, unreasonable rules. But even if your background is different, perhaps you can relate to the feelings that surface when you find yourself in situations where others are calling the shots, placing what seem to be unreasonable demands on you or making decisions that impact you without your input. You might sense that you aren't being given choices or that someone is overtly or covertly manipulating you. You feel controlled...and you feel angry.

That's what happened to Bob. There was a fire smoldering in him, and it was about to burst into flames. But, as a thirty-eight-year-old adult, he realized that his anger was self-defeating. He wanted to learn how to respond to his boss's attempts to micromanage him in a way that would extinguish the smoldering coals instead of fanning them into a flame.

The truth is that few of us like being controlled, and when we feel that we are, we usually become angry and resist by trying to reassert our own control. What are some ways we attempt to use control or counter-control strategies in our relationships?

It's fairly easy to spot overt tactics. They are visible when we are bossy, critical, highly defensive, or argumentative or when we speak in an intense tone of voice. Reminding, nagging, lecturing, giving unsolicited advice, screaming, begging, bribing, coercing, complaining, whining, insisting, criticizing, pressuring, intimidating, checking up on, forming coalitions, minding other people's business, dropping subtle and not-so-subtle hints, and interrogating are all signs that we are being controlling.

It's a bit harder to detect covert tactics, but they are just as real. They include withdrawing, avoiding, giving the silent treatment, pouting, or treating others with indifference. Some may feign helplessness and try to elicit pity from those around them. Others might hide behind a façade of spirituality and phony religious rhetoric. Whatever the strategy, the underlying goal is always the same: to make people do what we want them to do.

Whether we rely on these tactics to assert control over other people or to counter their attempts to control us, when we resort to them, we find ourselves caught in a vicious cycle that only generates more anger. I witnessed this in my relationship with our daughter one year when she was in high school.

Jessie had suffered an injury that not only sidelined her from a sport she deeply loved, but also led to several months of chronic pain that interrupted her sleep and made it difficult for her to concentrate in class. The stress depressed her immune system, and it seemed as though she caught every virus known to man that year. She missed classes for long stretches of time, and the makeup assignments piled high. The academic load of the honors classes she was taking completely overwhelmed her.

Wanting to be a good mom, I moved in to fix things. I scheduled times for us to work together on homework, collected handouts from teachers when Jessie was home sick, told her I would proofread her papers (after all, writing is my thing), offered to hire tutors (her advanced math classes were beyond John and me), talked with the school counselor, and did what I could do to help out.

There was one problem: Jessie didn't want me to fix things. She hadn't asked for my help, and she really wasn't interested in it. Actually, it was worse than that. She saw my efforts to help not as support but as pressure, and she flat-out resented it.

Of course, I was "only trying to help." I wanted to do my job as a responsible parent and make sure she was doing what she was supposed to do. I saw the bigger picture, knew things needed to change, and was bound and determined to change them. I tried all the positive reinforcement and bargaining strategies in the book, and, sad to say, I ended up making both of us miserable...and angry.

One afternoon I spoke with my mentor and told her about the frustration I felt about Jessie being behind in school. She had always been an honors student. This was new territory we hadn't traveled before, and it was scary. Wise woman that she is, my mentor said, "Your daughter is very bright. She isn't the kind of person who is going to do something simply because you think it's a good idea. She'll do something about this when she concludes for herself that it's a good idea. Even then, she may not want your help. Your efforts to 'help' are driving her away. Which is more important, your relationship with your daughter, or your daughter's grades?"

Ouch. I was nailed to the wall.

I realized that I had spent more time and energy trying to manage Jessie's academic performance than being sensitive to her more pressing personal needs. In her difficult time of loss, she needed more of my listening ear and less of my unsolicited advice.

Shortly after meeting with my mentor, I unloaded the burdens of my heart to God. I talked about my confusion as a mom and asked Him if I was doing too much, enough, or not enough to support Jessie. I wanted to find a healthy balance. His answer surprised me. In my mind I saw a big toolbox, brimming over with dozens of tools. Big tools. Little tools. Sharp ones. Dull ones. Straight. Crooked. Rough. Smooth. Every kind of tool imaginable. I sensed that the Lord wanted to impress me with this message: *You are only one tool in this toolbox. I am using many other tools to shape Jessie.*

I finally got the message: I needed to stop trying so hard and surrender Jessie to God. My control strategies were preventing me from loving and enjoying her as God desired. God was very aware of what was going on in her life, and He knew that her situation didn't require me to assert control as a part of discipline. In a kind way He asked me to step aside so that He could continue the good work He had begun in her. I did.

When the new school year began, Jessie discovered other activities she enjoyed and set some academic goals for herself. Because they were her decisions, things went much better. Both of us felt much less anger, and love flowed more freely between us. Releasing my grip on her freed both of us and allowed our lives to unfold more naturally.

When we think we can control others, we're only fooling ourselves. Eventually people will either resist our efforts, or they will redouble their own efforts to make the point that they will not be controlled. Nothing changes, and everyone ends up angry. If we take it upon ourselves to try to control others in order to get our own way, we will find ourselves irritable, agitated, hot-tempered, and, ultimately, out of control. Paul sums it up nicely:

It is obvious what kind of life develops out of *trying to get your own way all the time*: repetitive, loveless, cheap sex; a stinking accumulation of mental and emotional garbage; frenzied and joyless grabs for happiness; trinket gods; magic-show religion; paranoid loneliness; cutthroat competition; all-consuming-yet-never-satisfied wants; *a brutal temper; an impotence to love or be loved*; divided homes and divided lives; small-minded and lopsided pursuits; the vicious habit of depersonalizing everyone into a rival; *uncontrolled and uncontrollable* addictions; ugly parodies of community. I could go on. (Galatians 5:19-21, *The Message*)

We can make a better choice: We can bring our focus back to our own lives and concentrate on living life God's way. As Paul indicates, the results are far more rewarding:

But what happens when we live God's way? He brings gifts into our lives, much the same way that fruit appears in an orchard—things like affection for others, exuberance about life, serenity. We develop a willingness to stick with things, a sense of compassion in the heart, and a conviction that a basic holiness permeates things and people. We find ourselves involved in loyal commitments, *not needing to force our way in life, able to marshal and direct our energies wisely*.... Among those who belong to Christ, everything connected with *getting our own way* and mindlessly responding to what everyone else calls necessities is killed off for good—crucified.

Since this is the kind of life we have chosen, the life of the Spirit, let us make sure that we do not just hold it as an idea in our heads or a sentiment in our hearts, but work out its implications in every detail of our lives. That means we will not compare ourselves with each other as if one of us were better and another worse. We have far more interesting things to do with our lives. Each of us is an original. (vv. 22-26, *The Message*)

Notice how Paul makes the point that each person is unique? I have my place in this world, and you have yours. God doesn't ask me to carry out your assignments, and He doesn't ask you to carry out mine. Uniqueness necessitates differences. We need to focus on living the original, unique plan God designed for us, and we need to allow others the freedom to do the same.

Nowhere in the Bible are we told to try to control others. Nowhere does God instruct us to force what we think is best on them. The truth is that the only person God asks us to control is ourselves. We aren't to try to make others over in our image. The world doesn't need another John or Pam Vredevelt. It doesn't need another (fill in your name). But it does need people who are living God's way, daily being changed by the Holy Spirit to reflect God's image.

When Jesus was asked which was the greatest commandment, He replied: "'Love the Lord your God with all your passion and prayer and intelligence.' This is the most important, the first on any list. But there is a second to set alongside it: 'Love others as well as you love yourself'" (Matthew 22:37-39, *The Message*).

Note that the commandment that follows right on the heels of the first is *not* "Control others as you control yourself." We love others when we give them the freedom to make choices and learn from their mistakes and successes, free from our attempts to control them. It's the way God loves us, and it's the way He wants us to love others.

How do we let go of anger? We open our clenched fists and relinquish control. We turn things loose. We resist the temptation to play God and allow Him to reign without a rival.

In short, we let go.

Chapter Twenty-Three

RULE OUT BURNOUT

If you don't slow down, you'll break down.

JUDITH ST. PIERRE

Todd, a forty-year-old successful corporate executive, scheduled an appointment with John because he wanted to learn how to manage his anger. Todd's job had kept him driving himself at maximum speed for long hours, day after day, for years. By the time he sought counseling, he was living on the verge of burnout. He complained of fatigue and depression. He felt that life wasn't worth living, and he was sick and tired of being sick and tired.

"I work sixty hours a week and have never been more frustrated in all my life," he told John. "Everywhere I turn I have to put out another fire. If it's not one thing, it's another." He also complained of feeling irritable all the time.

Make no mistake: Overworked, stressed-out people are angry! They may not show it, but the chronic unmet need for rest and renewal steals their joy and leaves them feeling resentful. It's impossible to have sound physical, mental, and spiritual health if we deprive our bodies and ignore our basic needs. Making his job his highest priority had gradually destroyed any balance Todd might have had in his life and had left him feeling angry.

In a typical day, Todd's alarm went off at five o'clock in the morning, he was on his way to work by six, and he seldom walked back through the door at the end of the day before seven-thirty. After grabbing a quick bite to eat, he spent a few hours catching up on deskwork and reading e-mails before turning out the lights at eleven. When John asked Todd how he was able to stay awake at the office after only six hours sleep, he replied, "That's all the sleep anybody gets in my line of work. We just keep the coffee going all day."

I hear the same complaints from many top-level professionals, but they're not alone. It's a common dilemma. We live in a very fast-paced world that places heavy demands on us. Our daily planners are crammed with entries marked "Action Required," and there are never enough hours in a day to accomplish everything on our to-do lists. While this is true, we need to remember that sleep is one of the primary ways the body restores itself. If we rob ourselves of sleep by burning the candle at both ends, we will be irritable and easily angered.

Studies on sleep deprivation show that sleep is necessary for our brains to work efficiently, especially in the higher-level brain processes that sustain focused attention, concentration, and motivation. There is no question that a consistent pattern of sound sleep increases our ability to successfully manage the various stresses we experience in life.

It is also common knowledge that people who try to live on less than four or five hours of sleep for an ongoing period of time are at higher risk for dying. By living in 9-1-1 mode during most of his waking hours and not getting enough sleep at night, Todd was setting himself up for a stroke or a heart attack. The human body will endure extreme pressure only so long before it starts sending overload messages. Todd's perpetual irritability and depression were clear signs that the brain chemicals responsible for sustaining a good mood and clarity of thought were being severely taxed.

One of John's goals was to help Todd find a balance between fulfilling the demands of his job and meeting his physical needs. He encouraged Todd to give himself permission to take care of his body, not only by getting enough sleep, but also by routinely setting aside periods of time for exercise to reduce his stress.

Todd set small, incremental goals and gradually incorporated them into his daily routine. He began by setting limits on the number of hours he spent at the office so he could use the company's exercise facility after work. Instead of leaving the office at 7:00 p.m., he left somewhere between 5:00 and 6:00 in order to work out with weights, jog on the treadmill for thirty minutes, and shower before heading home. He tried to do this a minimum of three times a week.

If his day had been particularly stressful, on the drive home he listened to a relaxing instrumental CD instead of the usual talk show. He reduced the time he spent on desk work and the Internet after dinner and made an effort to be in bed by 9:30 p.m., which made it possible for him to get seven and a half hours of sleep before the alarm sounded at 5:00 a.m.

After several weeks of this new routine, Todd said that his energy level had increased, but he still complained that he felt depressed and irritable much of the time. In reviewing Todd's family history, John discovered that Todd's father and grandfather had also struggled with depression. He talked with Todd about the possibility that he had a genetic predisposition for depression, which for some people feels more like perpetual irritability and anger than a blue mood. At John's suggestion, Todd saw his physician, who prescribed an antidepressant for Todd to use for six to nine months.

The brain is like any other organ in the body: It can become impaired and not function properly for any of a number of reasons. We know that prolonged periods of stress can deplete the chemicals in the brain responsible for good mood, concentration, focus, motivation, sound sleep, and overall peace of mind. Medications such as the antidepressant that Todd's doctor prescribed work on the brain like a cast or a splint would work on a broken arm. They support the brain's nerve cells while a person is learning new, stress-reducing habits, and they enhance healing by bolstering the brain chemicals depleted by chronic stress.

John and I have heard people express fears about using antidepressant medicines. Some are concerned about becoming addicted; others fear that it will change their personalities. These are unfounded fears that perpetuate unnecessary suffering. When medications are judiciously and appropriately applied—not one size fits all—people can recover from depression.

Research shows that the majority of people treated with a combination of medication and cognitive behavior therapy experience marked improvement and relief. On the average, one-third of those taking medication can discontinue its use within nine to twelve months, another third will need to use it intermittently through life, and another third will benefit from ongoing use.

Let's go back to Todd and John. The first antidepressant Todd tried was overly sedating and caused some nausea, so the doctor prescribed a second medication, which ended up being just the right fit. Within a month, Todd's mood and motivation were much improved, and he was able to be more objective and less reactive on the job. Little problems didn't instantaneously become big problems in his mind as they had previously.

Todd's conscientious attention to his physical needs played an important role in his ability to overcome his pervasive irritability and anger. But John's work with Todd didn't stop with these basic strategies for physical self-care. He wanted to help Todd address his unmet spiritual needs, which were helping fuel the workaholic tendencies that resulted in his chronic fatigue and anger.

Todd had been so busy with work that he hadn't left time for his relationship with God. "I stopped going to church because I wanted to do things around the house on Sunday that I couldn't get done during the week," he told John.

"What kind of an impact has that choice had on you?" John asked.

After pausing to think, Todd replied, "It's left me feeling disconnected from God."

"Todd, you came in for counseling wanting to learn how to manage your anger. You're feeling better now because you're taking care of your physical needs. But your spiritual needs are equally important. Our frustration decreases and our peace of mind increases when we welcome God to participate in whatever we're involved in.

"God doesn't dispense strength and encouragement like a physician does medication. He doesn't give us something to 'take' to handle our anger. He gives us Himself. He says, 'Come to me, all you who are weary and burdened, and I will give you rest' (Matthew 11:28). God is our peace. He wants to give us rest. All He asks is that we come to Him, spend time with Him, talk to Him, and listen to His Spirit speak as we read the Scriptures. Might there be some ways you could invite God to be more involved in your life?"

Todd left his session with John that day challenged to think about how he could develop his relationship with God. He wanted God to become a higher priority in his life. During a period of reevaluation, he decided to set aside the first half-hour of the day to read a devotional Bible and pray. He also decided that before going to bed at night he would briefly review what he had read in the morning and remind himself of the thoughts that seemed particularly relevant to what was happening in his life. And, last but not least, he decided to release the concerns of his day into God's care before he went to sleep.

As the months passed, Todd grew stronger in his relationship with God, and his emotional composure improved as well. In taking care of his physical, mental, and spiritual needs, Todd increased his ability to tolerate the frustrations that came in the course of a normal day. He still found himself frustrated and angry at times, as we all do, but he didn't get stuck in his anger. Instead, he had the inner stamina to work through his aggravations, and he let his anger go.

Reclaim Your Life

FOOD FOR THOUGHT

Let us then approach the throne of grace with confidence,
so that we may receive mercy and find grace
to help us in our time of need.

HEBREWS 4:16

PRAYER FOR TODAY

Father, I don't want to be angry. Or rather, I don't want to feel like my anger controls me and defines my life. Please help me to understand my anger so that I can deal with it in a healthy and productive way. Please control the filter through which I view interactions and events. Lord, please remind me to seek the facts and your perspective of the facts. Lead me to the truth. In the places I am hurting and empty, Lord, please fill me with Your Spirit. Please show me fulfillment in You, and give me the power to seek the changes I need to make in my own heart and life. Lord, I ask all these things in Your name. Amen.

STEPS TO TAKE THIS MONTH

- Apply the ABC tool to a frustrating situation you recently experienced. You can reread the story about Larry and Karen if you need a jump start in applying the principle to your own life.

- Take a deep breath. What things do you need to give to God *right now*? If you don't already keep a journal, consider starting one so that you have a place to register your hurts and frustrations.

- Write down the PPP strategy—*pause, ponder,* and *pray*—and keep it somewhere handy to remind yourself of this principle when a situation arises in which you might need it.

- Think of a recent time when you were angry. Did a limited awareness of the facts fuel your fire? This month, as you interact with your spouse, family, or friends, remember this truth. When a situation arises that might normally spur anger, stop yourself and look at the *facts*.

- Think of a time when you fought the Pharisee within you and swallowed your pride. How did the Lord provide for your spirit?

- Reread Galatians 5:19–21 (on page 169). Have you reaped any of these things out of your attempt to control? How has it ultimately hurt you? Now read verses 22–26 (on pages 169–170). What can you do today to shift your focus to doing things *God's way*? Ask Him to give you the strength and determination to follow through.

- After reading through this section, do you see any unhealthy choices you are making or have made that might be linked to anger? What needs in your life feel unmet? Do you see ways that they could be met? Ask God to help you identify your options and to show you what to change in your own life—whether internal or external—to bring you to a place of fulfillment.

- Are you overworked and stressed out? Who isn't?! The more important question is, Are you doing something about it? This month, make it a priority to get at least seven hours of sleep each night, to eat balanced meals, and to take some time for yourself. If you're busy, this probably sounds like a lot! Just take small steps, and don't beat yourself up if you're not able to make these goals every day. After some time you'll begin to feel better, and it will become easier for you to take care of yourself.

RELEASE THOSE WHO HAVE HURT YOU

*The word "Comforter" as applied to the
Holy Spirit needs to be translated by some vigorous term.
Literally, it means "with strength." Jesus promised
his followers that "The Strengthener" would be with them.
This promise is no lullaby for the fainthearted.
It is a blood transfusion for courageous living.*

E. PAUL HOVEY

Chapter Twenty-Four

REQUEST
THE GIFT OF FAITH

A wise man once said, "Whatever came to me,
I looked on it as God's gift for some special purpose.
If it was a difficulty, I knew He gave it to me to struggle with,
to strengthen my mind and my faith." That idea has
sweetened and helped me all of my life.

ANONYMOUS

Though we live in a world filled with unexpected problems, unpredictable outcomes, and upsetting realities, worry and anxiety don't have to be the defining qualities of our lives. As we learn how to let go of these troubling emotions, confidence and peace of mind can govern our experiences. But these qualities don't come strictly from our own efforts; they also come as we trust. Brennan Manning, one of my favorite writers, says it well:

Like faith and hope, trust cannot be self-generated. I cannot simply *will* myself to trust. What outrageous irony: the one thing I am responsible for throughout my life I cannot generate. The one thing I need to do I cannot do. But such is the meaning of radical dependence. It consists in theological virtues, in divinely ordained gifts.[1]

One morning shortly after Nathan was born, I came across a passage in the Bible that spoke of these divinely ordained gifts. I had read these paragraphs many times before, but on that particular morning the words carried new meaning for me:

Now there are different kinds of spiritual gifts, but it is the same Holy Spirit who is the source of them all.... A spiritual gift is given to each of us as a means of helping the entire church.

To one person the Spirit gives the ability to give wise advice; to another he gives the gift of special knowledge. The Spirit gives special faith to another, and to someone else he gives the power to heal the sick.... It is the one and only Holy Spirit who distributes these gifts. (1 Corinthians 12:4, 7–9, 11, NLT)

I already knew that I had a measure of faith. But these verses talk about a special spiritual gift of faith imparted by the Spirit of God that goes beyond the norm. In this context it's a faith that enables a person to be fully persuaded by and completely reliant on the truthfulness of God. It is faith that facilitates trust.

I want this, Lord! I exclaimed to myself. *My emotions are getting the best of me. I need Your Spirit to give me faith. It says here that You give special faith to some. I want all You have to give, Lord.*

I can't tell you that all my fears dissolved with that brief prayer, but I can tell you that I began to sense a greater propensity in my spirit to believe God for whatever I needed at any given time. As I continued to replenish my spirit and open my heart to the Lord, my anxiety became more manageable. In the process it became very clear to me that faith and fear are powerful opposites.

Faith doesn't necessarily make all of our fears disappear, but it does empower us to be people of courage who can tolerate distress and cope with life's hardships.

Earlier in this book I mentioned an acrostic for the word *fear*: False Evidence Appearing Real. I decided to develop an acrostic for the word *faith* to use when I was caught in the crossfire of scary thoughts: Fully Abandoned (to God) In Trust (and) Humility. When I'm facing trials and tribulations and I'm vulnerable to those gnawing what ifs, I need to activate my faith. I need to tilt my head heavenward, raise my hands in surrender, and say, *God, no matter what, I am fully abandoned to You in trust and humility.*

This was a posture I sensed in a man whose faith caused Jesus to marvel. You can read about him in the book of Matthew:

When Jesus had entered Capernaum, a centurion came to him, asking for help. "Lord," he said, "my servant lies at home paralyzed and in terrible suffering."

Jesus said to him, "I will go and heal him."

The centurion replied, "Lord, I do not deserve to have you come under my roof. But just say the word, and my servant will be healed. For I myself am a man under authority, with soldiers under me. I tell this one, 'Go,' and he goes; and that one, 'Come,' and he comes. I say to my servant, 'Do this,' and he does it."

When Jesus heard this, he was astonished and said to those following him, "I tell you the truth, I have not found anyone in Israel with such great faith."

Then Jesus said to the centurion, "Go! It will be done just as you believed it would." And his servant was healed at that very hour. (Matthew 8:5–10, 13)

I read this story through several times and wondered what Jesus saw in this man's heart. He wasn't a religious leader. He wasn't even a Jew. He was a Roman soldier. Think about it: For years Jesus had mixed with the most religious people of His day. He had rubbed shoulders with prominent Old Testament scholars. He had personally trained and mentored a select few. But these verses say that Jesus had not met anyone in Israel with such astounding faith.

Do you know that there are only two places in the Bible where Jesus is amazed at anything? One is in this text. The other is where Jesus marvels at the unbelief of the people in His hometown.

I searched the story to find out why the man had received such an accolade. He doesn't appear to have done anything. Jesus' disciples had been performing mind-boggling miracles among the crowds, yet the Lord didn't single out any of them as having tremendous faith. What did Jesus see in this soldier?

I think one answer lies in the soldier's response to Jesus. The story says that this Roman soldier called him "Lord." That may not seem like a big deal to you, but back then it was politically incorrect—a full-fledged no-no! Understanding the historical context is critical.

From numerous records we know that at the time all Roman citizens were required to revere the emperor as their lord. Anything to the contrary invited severe punishment. This Roman soldier was well aware of the laws of the day. After all, he helped the emperor enforce them. He knew that when he publicly addressed Jesus as "Lord," he was risking his life by calling someone other than the emperor by that title. Punishment for this infraction ranged from loss of rank to execution.

This particular Roman soldier was an officer of high rank who had trained and worked diligently for years to attain his status. Now he was wealthy and powerful. Yet, with a few public words about Jesus, he risked losing everything, including his life. The soldier's comment demonstrated total abandonment, complete trust, and absolute humility before the One he addressed as "Lord."[2]

Scores of people stood around Jesus and the soldier that day. Many believed that Jesus could work miracles. But those seeking only the miraculous didn't impress Him. Instead, He marveled at a man who, through enormous faith, was willing to trust Him with everything.

What the story of the Roman soldier says to me is that God doesn't want first place in my life; He wants all of my life. He wants me to abandon myself totally to Him. He wants me to confidently, actively believe in His ability to care for me.

Brennan Manning describes this attitude of the heart beautifully:

Abba, into your hands I entrust my body, mind, and spirit and this entire day—morning, afternoon, evening, and night. Whatever you want of me, I want of me, falling into you and trusting you in the midst of my life. Into your heart I entrust my heart, feeble, distracted, insecure, uncertain. God, unto you I abandon myself in Jesus our Lord. Amen.[3]

This is the attitude we need when we are suffering hardship or emerging from the shadows of a dark time of stress, our confidence shaken. Overwhelming pressures can break down our defenses and create a crisis of faith. When we're flooded with anxiety, we can find ourselves asking questions that would otherwise be unthinkable:

Where is God?

Does God love me?

Is God really in control?

How can anything good possibly come out of something so bad?

Anxiety distorts our perceptions. Worry burns up a tremendous

amount of mental and emotional energy. If you have recently suffered from worry and anxiety, please give yourself grace. Give
yourself time to process your thoughts and feelings. And give God
time to restore your bearings.

It has been many years since Nathan entered this world. I still
frequently ask God to grant me the gift of faith. The practice of surrendering to His ways and purposes is becoming more habitual.
When worries surface, prompting me to forecast negatively, I calm
myself down by making statements of faith.

Remember, the battle of faith against fear is waged in the mind.
Fearful thoughts agitate the body. Faith-filled thoughts bring peace.
I'll show you what I mean.

When you're in the middle of adversity:
Fear says, "God has left you. He doesn't care.
     You're on your own."
Faith says, "In God's kingdom everything
     is based on promise, not on feeling.
     God has a plan, and it is built on love."

When someone has ripped you off:
Fear says, "You can't trust people."
Faith says, "God, the Redeemer, restores stolen goods
     to their rightful owners, one way or another."

When you're slandered:
Fear says, "Everyone is talking.
     Your reputation is smeared for life."
Faith says, "God will straighten the record
     when false things have been said about me."

When you've made a major blunder:
Fear says, "It's over. You've blown it.
    You may as well throw in the towel."
Faith says, "Failure is always an event, never a person.
    God will use my strengths and my weaknesses
    to accomplish His plans."

When you're waiting for something:
Fear says, "You're going to be on hold forever."
Faith says, "My time is in God's hands.
    He will accomplish His plans for me right on schedule."

When you ask God for something, and He says no:
Fear says, "If God really loved you,
    He would give you what you want."
Faith says, "God is acting for my highest good."

When you fail:
Fear says, "You can't trust God.
    Look at how He's let you down."
Faith says, "God has proven His trustworthiness
    by dying for me."

When you're staggering under a load of guilt:
Fear says, "Your mistakes will haunt you for the rest
    of your life."
Faith says, "God holds nothing against me.
    He has sovereignly declared me pardoned."

When you face stinging regret:
Fear says, "Your scars limit you."
Faith says, "I am useful to God, not in spite of my scars,
　　but because of them."

When a friend has let you down:
Fear says, "Why bother? It's not worth going on."
Faith says, "God will take the wrongs others have done me
　　and use them for my ultimate good."

When you experience the pruning of God's shears:
Fear says, "If God loved you, He wouldn't
　　let you suffer like this."
Faith says, "God knows what I need better than I do.
　　Even Christ learned obedience through what He suffered."

Friend, our overwhelming emotions don't intimidate God. Nor do our feelings influence God's responses—but our faith does.

Let's allow our anxieties to be a reminder of our need to sur-render—to abandon ourselves fully to God in trust and humility. Let's use worry to trigger a prayer:

God, please birth the gift of faith in my spirit today. Help me to believe in ways I have not yet believed. Exchange my spirit of fear for a spirit of faith. Open the eyes of my heart to see the differ-ences that the gifts of Your Spirit are making in my life—today.

On the heels of that kind of prayer, I hope we will give the Lord some more opportunities to marvel.

Chapter Twenty-Five

RESPOND
TO GOD'S VOICE

*My friends, be glad, even if you have a lot of trouble.
You know that you learn to endure by having your faith tested.
If any of you need wisdom, you should ask God,
and it will be given to you.*

JAMES 1:2–3, 5, CEV

When we find ourselves in turmoil because someone has hurt us, one way to reduce the aggressive, destructive element of our anger is to listen to God's voice and respond immediately to what He tells us. His perspectives will enable us to feel our feelings and still not blow it.

Every arena of life has its share of "difficult" people. We've all brushed shoulders with them: "tanks, snipers, exploders, complainers, bulldozers, wet blankets, silent clams, procrastinators, and know-it-alls."[1] And, if we are honest, we'll admit that at one time or another we've probably adopted one or more of these roles ourselves and been someone else's difficult person.

When we come into conflict with difficult people, our natural human tendency is to strive for a position of apparent superiority. Instead of treating them with reason and respect, we seek to get the upper hand and press them under our thumbs by sending cues that say "I'm better than you are." As Dr. Les Carter and Dr. Frank Minirth point out, this natural tendency to relate to others strictly on the basis of their performance only produces more anger:

> In any arena, be it job performance, emotional management, social skills, or Christian living, we feel compelled to grade the performance. Implied in any evaluation, no matter how positive, is the covertly communicated threat, "You'd better keep up the high performance or I'll be forced to tell you how bad you are." A strong emphasis on evaluation coupled with the inevitable inability for any of us to be perfect leads head-on to frustration and anger.[2]

When we act on our first impulses, we are prone to surrender to the unbridled desires of our darker sides and act on shallow urges and fleeting passions rather than on our deeper values and convictions. For example, if your son criticizes your viewpoint, instead of speaking to him with respect you might tell him that he doesn't have a clue. If a coworker doesn't do things exactly the way you would, you make it your job to convey the message that he or she doesn't measure up. If your spouse can talk circles around you, you choose not to enter a discussion. This response to our anger, if allowed to dominate our interactions with others, will destroy our relationships and us.

Ultimately, it boils down to this: When we're angry, we have to make a decision. Are we going to handle things ourselves, or are we going to ask God to speak to us? All God needs from us is an invitation and ten seconds—ten seconds in which we tune in to Him and ask, *What do You want me to do? What do You want me to see? Show me. Lead me.* Successful anger management depends on our ability to rely on God for whatever we need, whenever we need it. It comes as we yield to Him and ask Him to speak.

God has a provision for every conflict we encounter. The bigger the problem, the bigger God's provision. When we ask the Holy Spirit to enlighten us, to give us His perspective, and to guide us and empower our responses, we are more likely to appropriately express our anger and use it for good. The question is, Are we going to tap into what God has to offer or try to muscle through on our own?

Jesus made it clear that if we ask for God's provision we will receive it:

> "Ask and it will be given to you; seek and you will find; knock and the door will be opened to you. For everyone who asks receives; he who seeks finds; and to him who knocks, the door will be opened. Which of you fathers, if your son asks for a fish, will give him a snake instead? Or if he asks for an egg, will give him a scorpion? If you then, though you are evil, know how to give good gifts to your children, how much more will your Father in heaven give the Holy Spirit to those who ask him!" (Luke 11:9–13)

In the heat of a conflict our natural human impulses can prompt us in directions that are completely opposite of where the Holy Spirit would lead us. He will never advise us to engage in one-upmanship or prompt us to demean those who make mistakes or show signs of imperfection. He won't stir us up to manipulate circumstances to get even.

When we ask the Holy Spirit to rule our minds, wills, and emotions, our responses to problematic issues will reflect His nature. He will guide us to value and treat others with a spirit of humility. He will lead us to speak in ways that are governed by reason, respect, and kindness. He will give us grace-filled eyes that focus on the tremendous intrinsic value and worth of each individual. He will press us to affirm others in their strengths and to assist them in their areas of weakness while speaking the truth in love. He will infuse our words and actions with "love, joy, peace, patience, kindness, goodness, faithfulness, gentleness and self-control" (Galatians 5:22-23). This is how good overcomes evil.

The bottom line is that we need God's help. We simply do not have God's ability to properly judge every situation accurately. We are limited in our understanding, in our courage, and in our ability to respond constructively to the harsh realities of life. That is why God gave us the Holy Spirit to be our companion, guide, and ongoing power supply. His resources are always sufficient and never ending.

I recall an occasion when the Holy Spirit gave John explicit instructions during an emotionally charged encounter with a difficult person, whom I'll call Cal. On several occasions when John and I were in Cal's company, I noticed some signs that Cal harbored ill feelings toward John. One time, John and I were in a room with a couple dozen other people. When one of the men in the group asked John to pray for him about something specific, I saw Cal surreptitiously roll his eyes and smirk. On another occasion I was casually chatting with Cal and a few others when John approached the group. Looking right past him, Cal abruptly left. I said nothing but asked God to bring to light whatever was necessary for harmony to prevail.

A few weeks later someone confided to me that Cal had been talking about John in a negative fashion. When I heard this I immediately became angry. *Why doesn't Cal talk to John directly if there's a problem?* I asked myself. I asked God what He wanted me to do with this troublesome information, and He said, *Nothing! Be quiet and pray.* So that's what I did. Again I asked the Spirit of God to bring out into the open whatever needed to be revealed.

God answered that prayer. Shortly thereafter, when John was in a meeting with Cal and several other people, Cal lashed out at him. With his voice raised and his eyes flaming, he castigated John for an error he had made while carrying out a certain task. When Cal continued to blast away, John asked, "Cal, why are you getting so angry?"

Cal's red-faced response was, "I'm not angry! You should have told us..." Although John had admitted his error and committed himself to correcting the problem in the future, Cal's condescending comments continued.

John wanted to defend himself. It was humiliating to be attacked in front of his peers, and he felt like confronting Cal about his patronizing, "I'll show you who's better" attitude. But at that point, John sensed the Holy Spirit saying, *Be quiet. Don't defend yourself.* Cal's reaction was disproportionate to the infraction, and it occurred to John that something else might be fueling Cal's anger.

When the meeting was over, John asked Cal if he would meet with him to talk further. Cal was noncommittal. John waited a few days and then approached Cal a second time with a request that they meet over coffee. Cal put him off again, saying he would call John to schedule a time to meet. The call never came. A week later, John asked Cal a third time to get together, and finally Cal agreed.

When they met, John opened the discussion. "Cal, I know you're angry with me," he said, "and I want to understand why."

Much to John's surprise, Cal replied, "I've done a lot of thinking and praying about this, and I think I've been angry with you because I feel insecure and don't think you respect my position or support me."

"Is there anything that I've done that has made you think I'm not behind you?" John asked.

"No," Cal replied, shaking his head and looking at the floor. "I think this has more to do with me than it does with you."

John reassured Cal that he did respect him and his role. He affirmed his gifts and talents and told him that his contributions were invaluable. At the close of their time together they prayed for each other and embraced. The breach was repaired and unity was restored.

This never would have happened if both John and Cal hadn't been willing to follow through with what the Holy Spirit was leading them to do. John's instructions were to be quiet, to not defend himself, and to make an effort to understand. Cal's were to be emotionally honest and to admit his insecurities. When both men relied on the Spirit to lead, reconciliation occurred.

Sad to say, endings like this are not the norm. Far more relationships end in big blowouts over small issues because angry people don't rely on the Holy Spirit to guide them. Instead of inviting God to direct, they allow their emotions to rule. And when they do, the results can have a destructive impact on everyone involved.

One of the good things about struggling with anger is that it can help us see that we weren't built to live our lives apart from God. As we commune with the Holy Spirit and cultivate an intimate friendship with Him, He promises to give us whatever we need to respond to the challenges we face.

There is absolutely no frustration in your life that God doesn't know about. There is no difficulty that He can't help you handle, no aggravation that He can't use to teach you something about yourself. And there's no hardship that can't teach you something about God's goodness, faithfulness, and provision for your life. When you don't know the way but you know the Guide, you can have every confidence that He will order your steps and find a way through whatever problems are at hand. When you walk with God, you will get where He's going.

When you listen to God's voice and respond accordingly, God gives you grace and power and facilitates deep, long-lasting, positive change inside you—regardless of what is happening outside you. As you open-handedly offer your limited resources to God, He will do unlimited things. Good anger management isn't all up to you. It's a God-sized task, and rest assured, my friend, the Holy Spirit will give you what you need when you need it so you can manage your anger effectively and eventually let it go.

Chapter Twenty-Six

RENOUNCE REPLAYS AND REVENGE

He who seeks revenge digs two graves.

Just a year ago, Kevin had a good life.

A friendly, middle-class, law-abiding American, he works as a welder in town. He enjoyed a warm relationship with his wife, worked a steady job from seven to three, and attended his children's Little League games on weekends.

But one morning on his way to work, everything changed.

It was early, and Kevin's car was the only one on the road. As he approached a stop sign, he saw a pedestrian standing on the sidewalk. He thought the man was waiting to cross the street, so he rolled to a complete stop and motioned to him to go ahead. But the pedestrian shook his head and waved for him to pass. Kevin smiled, nodded, took a sip of his coffee, and pressed the accelerator. Just as he began moving forward, the man stepped toward the car, fell down, and started screaming, "You hit me! You hit me!"

Kevin knew that the car hadn't touched the man, but he got out to check. When two other cars approached, the scam artist was hollering as if a truck going fifty miles an hour had hit him.

Today, Kevin is in the midst of a messy lawsuit. Although he knows that he's innocent, the memory of the incident haunts him.

He hates the man for making his life a nightmare, and in an instinctive backlash against the one who is hurting him, he replays—over and over—the mental tape of that awful morning. Images of revenge energize him. He envisions finding the guy's house and setting it on fire. He fantasizes about hiring a hit man to take him out. Kevin is suffering, and he wants his offender to suffer too.

These images of revenge are dangerous and can be deadly if allowed to run their course. Kevin can't eat. He can't sleep. He's like a ticking time bomb waiting to explode at the slightest hint that he will be the victim of another injustice.

Deep down, he's afraid of what he might do.

Most of us have found ourselves struggling with images of retribution after we've been wounded. "Treason!" we cry, and pictures of how we can get even flash before our eyes. Consider the following examples:

- A coworker tells me that I should be promoted to take on a certain task and then tells my superior that I'm not good enough to do the job. I imagine suggesting that he make hypocrisy the topic of his next Bible study.

- A trusted friend betrays your confidence and tells a person known to be a gossip something that you wanted to remain private. Now "everybody" knows. You see yourself backing your betrayer into a corner, giving her a vicious tongue-lashing, and then walking out on her for good.

- A wife sarcastically puts down her husband in front of dinner company. He envisions slapping her to set her straight.

- A father discovers that his thirty-year-old brother has been sexually assaulting his six-year-old daughter. He envisions his hands around his brother's throat.

- A husband watches reruns of two planes smashing into the World Trade Center where his wife was at work on September 11, 2001. He pictures himself bombing Muslim communities.

Bottom line? Replays don't divert anger; they sustain and fuel it. Our minds play reruns of those wretched events over and over and over again, and many of the replays are laced with fantasies of retribution. With each painful image, our dreams of retaliation grow crueler, and the chance that we will act on our anger increases. Every angry scene we relive pushes the adrenaline button in our bodies and throws us into 911 mode all over again.

The more we rehearse our pain and fantasize revenge, the more we weaken our ability to control our impulses and set ourselves up to act in ways that can destroy us. Thoughts of being burned, cheated, and demeaned drive feelings of anger, humiliation, and hate...and they trap us in a torture chamber of our own making.

But we don't have to live at the mercy of the violent images that keep us chained to our pain. We don't have to be victimized by runaway fantasies that poison our souls with bitterness and hate. There's a way to put an end to the hostile nightmares. There's an alternative to clinging to our lust for revenge.

It's called *forgiveness*.

Rehearsing our offenders' evil deeds simply generates more evil in us. And one thing is certain: We cannot overcome evil with evil; we can only overcome evil with good. God is good, and He instructs us to forgive—not for His sake, but for ours. He knows that forgiveness is in our best interest and that it will work for our highest good.

Forgiveness and letting go of anger are one and the same. If we do not forgive, we sentence ourselves to a life imprisoned by pain. We freeze ourselves in the past, weigh ourselves down with heavy grudges, and become arrested in our grief. And we give our betrayers more power than they deserve by allowing them to repeatedly frustrate and immobilize us.

Does forgiveness come easily?

Frankly, it can be one of the most agonizing, difficult things we ever do.

Sometimes the mere *thought* of forgiving a person who has wounded us can make us angry. We don't want to forgive because we don't want to let them off the hook. In a twisted sort of way, we're prone to think that our unforgiving spirit somehow holds our offenders accountable for their wrong and keeps them from wounding us again. We fear that if we forgive we will be hurt again.

A husband whose wife had had an affair told John, "If I forgive her, she'll do it again." He was under the illusion that his lack of forgiveness was making her "toe the line" and keeping her in the marriage. But nothing could have been further from the truth. By hanging on to his anger, he was turning into a contemptuous crank and making it more likely that his wife would leave him. If we believe that there are benefits to not forgiving, we deceive ourselves.

Forgiveness is not easy or natural. It is difficult and supernatural. It requires God's involvement. The more we've been hurt, the more we need God to enable us to forgive. Deeper wounds require greater grace. Forgiveness is a process, and in each step there are two parts: our part and God's part. As we do ours, He does His. Walking through these steps—following the acronym F-O-R-G-I-V-E—with the Holy Spirit will give you the help you need to forgive those who have hurt you.

F: Face the Facts

OUR PART

We face our explosive sense of injustice and admit that we have been rehearsing the wrongs done to us. We acknowledge that these obsessions have fueled our anger and hate. We admit our powerlessness to let go of our anger, and we ask God to forgive us for the ill will we have felt toward others.

GOD'S PART

God forgives us. His Word assures us that this is so. "A broken and contrite heart, O God, you will not despise" (Psalm 51:17). "If we admit our sins—make a clean breast of them—he won't let us down; he'll be true to himself. He'll forgive our sins and purge us of all wrongdoing" (1 John 1:9, *The Message*).

O: Obstruct Thoughts of Revenge

OUR PART

When memories of our pain are triggered—as they will be—and we are tempted to envision revenge, we take control and immediately stop this mental process. We capture our thoughts and make them work for us instead of against us. One way to divert these violent thoughts is to boldly say, "Stop! It's not my job to balance the scales; it's God's job. Let it go!" We believe God when He says, "It is mine to avenge; I will repay" (Hebrews 10:30).

GOD'S PART

God keeps His promises; He will do what He says He will do. He will hold all of us, including those who have wounded us, accountable. "Each of us will give an account of himself to God" (Romans 14:12).

R: Relinquish Your Will

OUR PART

Next, we ask God to do what we cannot do. We pray, *God, I cannot forgive, but I am willing to be willing. Give me Your heart and mind in this situation. Help me perceive the one who hurt me from Your perspective. Do a creative work in my heart that will enable me to let go of my anger. Lead me to the place of understanding and empathy that Jesus experienced when He prayed on behalf of His murderers: "Father, forgive them, for they know not what they do"* (Luke 23:34, KJV).

GOD'S PART

In response to our cries for help, God promises to change us. He softens our stubborn, defensive hearts by the power of His Spirit within us. He says, "*I will* give them an undivided heart and put a new spirit in them; *I will* remove from them their heart of stone and give them a heart of flesh" (Ezekiel 11:19).

G: Grant Them Forgiveness

OUR PART

We do what the apostle Paul tells us to do: "Be...quick to forgive an offense. Forgive as quickly and completely as the Master forgave you" (Colossians 3:13, *The Message*). We make a deliberate choice to forgive those who have hurt us, and we name the date and time we do it. This has nothing to do with feelings or emotions. It is a tough-minded decision of the will.

GOD'S PART

Over time, God heals our emotions. God "heals the brokenhearted and binds up their wounds" (Psalm 147:3). He restores, renews, and refreshes us until our feelings catch up with our mental assent to let the anger go.

I: Inspect Yourself

OUR PART

We shift our focus away from those who have hurt us and concentrate on being who God wants *us* to be.

> "Do not judge, or you too will be judged. For in the same way you judge others, you will be judged, and with the measure you use, it will be measured to you. Why do you look at the speck of sawdust in your brother's eye and pay no attention to the plank in your own eye? How can you say to your brother, 'Let me take the speck out of your eye,' when all the time there is a plank in your own eye? You hypocrite, first take the plank out of your own eye, and then you will see clearly to remove the speck from your brother's eye." (Matthew 7:1–5)

GOD'S PART

As we keep our focus on being who God wants us to be, the qualities of His character increase in us, and our negative traits decrease. He gives us new perspectives laced with humility, understanding, and empathy, and these insights lead to new feelings. "Love comes from God" (1 John 4:7, *The Message*), and His love gradually eclipses our anger.

V: Validate Their Worth

OUR PART

We pray for those who have hurt us. "Pray for those who persecute you" (Matthew 5:44). If we don't know where to start, we ask God or someone we trust to guide us.

GOD'S PART

God teaches us how to pray for those who have hurt us. He gives us the words to say. He gives us the power to release others from our judgment whenever our pain resurfaces.

E: Exercise Compassion

OUR PART

We bless those who hurt us. "No retaliation. No sharp-tongued sarcasm. Instead, bless—that's your job, to bless. You'll be a blessing and also get a blessing" (1 Peter 3:9, *The Message*).

GOD'S PART

God blesses us with His goodness and favor in ways we never imagined or expected. "Whoever wants to embrace life and see the day fill up with good, here's what you do: say nothing evil or hurtful; snub evil and cultivate good; run after peace for all you're worth. God looks on all this with approval, listening and responding well to what he's asked" (1 Peter 3:10–12, *The Message*).

EVEN WITH THE HELP OF THE HOLY SPIRIT, it takes time to get through these steps. Forgiveness is not an instantaneous event. Progress in healing occurs in inches, not miles. It's typically a very slow process that rarely happens as smoothly or as quickly as we'd like. But the day will come when we're able to bless those who curse us, and when it does we can know that we have a forgiving spirit.

Our friend Graham comes to mind. Graham is a gifted teacher and educator who travels internationally speaking on a variety of subjects. Years ago, reports began filtering back to him that a prominent preacher of an independent church in town was publicly ridiculing him.

The verbal assaults continued week after week, and people in the community made it their business to tell Graham what was being said.

Months later, news came that this bad-mouthing preacher was losing people from his congregation and that the church was struggling to survive. Graham's loyal friends said to him, "Hey, that guy's getting what he deserves! God is taking revenge on him for the way he's been attacking you. Aren't you glad?"

But Graham wasn't glad. He was grieved because he knew that other innocent people were being hurt as things fell apart. It didn't make him happy to see relationships ruined and people left out in the cold.

God, what do You want me to do? Graham prayed. *How do You want me to respond to this one who is cursing me?*

An idea came to mind: *Pay his salary.*

But, God! Graham argued. *He would never take a penny from me! He hates everything about me.*

Another thought came: *Then do it in a way that he won't know it's from you.*

Graham followed that prompting. For many months he traveled across town in the middle of the night and dropped an envelope of cash through the mail slot of the preacher's front door. Before he left, he asked God to bless the man, his home, and his family. No one knew and no one found out. The blessing was between Graham and God.

Reports of the accusations against Graham gradually ceased, and one day he crossed paths with his adversary at a citywide meeting for ministers. When Graham asked him how things were going for him, the man admitted that he was struggling.

"Is there any way I can help you?" Graham asked.

Visibly shaken, the man hung his head. Then, breaking the awkward silence, he said, "I need to apologize to you. I have a big mouth." Graham put his arms around the man and embraced him while he wept. Since that day the two have been friends.

When others hurt you in ways you don't deserve, at some point you will come to the crossroad of decision. You'll have to look your pain square in the face and ask, *Am I going to hang on to my anger and do violence to myself, or am I going to forgive those who have wounded me and let the anger go?*

Are you ready to stop doing violence to yourself? If so, commit yourself to taking the steps that will enable you to forgive. You might find this symbolic exercise useful in sealing your commitment:

Think about one person who has hurt you. Imagine yourself taking the angry images and vengeful thoughts that you've had toward that person and putting them in both of your hands. Now close your hands and clench them tight. Focus on those clenched fists. Notice the pain and throbbing in your hands. All those ugly obsessions and resulting emotions are there in your tight grip.

Now lift your fists as high as you can toward heaven and open your hands before God. Give Him everything: Your anger. Your hate. Your bitterness. Your lust for revenge. Then offer Him your life. Your mind. Your will. Your emotions. Your agenda. Your past. Your present. Your future. All of it. Give it all up to Him. Let it go.

Do this again and again, seventy times seven, if the need arises.

Peter asked, "Lord, how often shall my brother sin against me and I forgive him? Up to seven times?" Jesus said to him, "I do not say to you, up to seven times, but up to seventy times seven" (Matthew 18:21-22, NASB). What this verse says to me is that we will find ourselves in difficult situations where we will have to forgive again and again and again. Forgiveness is a discipline we must practice on a regular basis. But as we do our part, God will always do His. When we relax our grip and open our hands to Him, we will give Him a new place to deposit whatever we need to let our anger go.

Reclaim Your Life

FOOD FOR THOUGHT

{Jesus said,} *"Are you tired? Worn out? Burned out on religion?
Come to me. Get away with me and you'll recover your life.
I'll show you how to take a real rest. Walk with me and work
with me—watch how I do it. Learn the unforced rhythms of grace.
I won't lay anything heavy or ill-fitting on you. Keep company
with me and you'll learn to live freely and lightly.*

MATTHEW 11:28–30, THE MESSAGE

PRAYER FOR TODAY

*Dear God, I acknowledge today that my past is just that: past. And yet
even though I realize this truth, sometimes my emotions tell me otherwise. I dwell on the things I want most to forget, and I suffer the
consequences. I don't want to hold onto the past anymore! Lord, please
help me to let go. Please guide me in forgiveness and remind me of Your
goodness and faithfulness. In Jesus' name, amen.*

STEPS TO TAKE THIS MONTH

- Do you want more confidence and peace of mind?
  This requires letting go as well as trusting the Lord.
  Open your heart to His Spirit and ask Him for faith.
  Reread the story of the centurion in Matthew 8:5–13.
  Call Him *"Lord"* and wait for the peace of mind only
  He can bring to follow. Journal examples of this
  throughout the month.

- Think of a difficulty or hardship from your past that
  showed you God's goodness, faithfulness, and provi-

208

sion in your life. Praise Him for that right now. And ask Him to show you the way—and more of Himself—through whatever situation you are struggling with right now.

- Are you harboring feelings of revenge toward someone? Or replaying negative interactions over and over? *Forgive.* Give God your anger, hate, bitterness, and desire for revenge and ask Him to take them from you forever.

PREPARE
FOR YOUR
TOMORROWS

*All of us can take steps — no matter how small
and insignificant at the start — in the
direction we want to go.*

MARSHA SINETAR

Chapter Twenty-Seven

REVISE EXPECTATIONS

Those who dwell continually upon their
expectations are apt to become oblivious to the
requirements of their actual situation.

CHARLES SANDERS PIERCE

*T*his morning I went for a sanity walk with a friend. She is a faithful, devoted mother of four children who has known the deep disappointment of unrealized dreams. "From the time my kids were little, I expected them to finish high school, attend college, and start families," she told me. "I didn't have any lofty dreams that any of them would be the president of the United States or the first astronaut to set foot on another planet. I just expected the basics.

"My husband and I were devastated when our oldest son started experimenting with drugs and dropped out of high school. Even though we had taught him well about the dangers of substance abuse, he chose to ignore us and go his own way. When our second son fathered a child out of wedlock, our expectations were shattered all over again. We had hoped that grandchildren would come along after the children were married, not before. Things didn't turn out anything like we had expected, and letting go of the dreams we had for our boys has been one of the most painful experiences we've ever endured."

"So how did you do it?" I asked her. "How did you let go?" It was obvious to me that, for the most part, she was on the other side of the debilitating grief, no longer incapacitated by the pain. I wondered what had helped usher her to that place of peace.

She referred me to a story in the Bible. "Do you remember the story of Abraham and Isaac?"

I nodded, for I knew the story well.

"Do you remember how Abraham placed Isaac on the altar and offered him up to God?"

"Yes," I replied, seeing the image in my mind.

"Well, that's what I had to do. As clearly as if it happened yesterday, I remember when, years ago, I cupped my hands in front of me, pictured my boys in my palms, and lifted them up to God. I told Him, *I place my boys in Your hands. They're Yours. You take over. Please fulfill Your plans for their lives.* I realized that our job of helping direct their course was done, because they were not open to our input.

"From that point on our expectations changed. We decided that we would do our best to love and support the boys in practical ways but that the results were between them and God."

I thought about my friend's words and the many times I too had placed my children in God's hands. I'll probably be praying those kinds of prayers until the Lord decides it's time for me to come home. It hurts to see your kids struggle and take hard knocks. For me, comfort comes from knowing that grasping, clinging, and hanging on with white-knuckled fists doesn't help. But letting go and placing whatever is troubling me into God's loving care does.

As an approach to meeting our needs, letting go is very different from clamping down, striving, and trying harder.

Not long ago I was sitting in my counseling office with a client who was confused and conflicted about a number of things going on in her life. In passing she mentioned that she had attended a funeral for a little boy with Down syndrome who had died of leukemia. She didn't know that my son was handicapped or that when Nathan was born we were told there is a higher incidence of leukemia among those with Down syndrome than there is for the typical population.

She had no idea what strong emotion her story stirred in me.

For the moment, I did the clinical thing. I suppressed the emotion and focused on helping my client. But, as most of us know, suppressed emotion doesn't stay down for long. It's like trying to hold a beach ball under water. No matter what you do, it keeps popping up.

I succeeded in pushing this woman's story to the back of my mind until the next evening, when I was sitting by the fire reading my mail. Among the stack of papers there was a letter from a woman who had read my book *Angel Behind the Rocking Chair*. She recounted some of the beautiful characteristics of her son, whom she had recently lost after a long battle with leukemia. The child had had Down's syndrome and was Nathan's age.

Well, that did it. I was overcome with emotion. All the feelings of the previous day came flooding back. At such times one thing is certain: No amount of striving or trying harder is going to resolve those deep conflicts of the soul.

I went to my bedroom, sat on the bed, had a hard cry, and talked to God. I told Him about my fears and asked Him to help me live in the here and now and not to forecast negatively into the future. And then I said something I don't think I had ever formally said before: *God, I choose to trust You with Nathan's life and with Nathan's death.* It was a statement of letting go that ushered in a sense of peace. My emotions weren't at flood stage anymore. They had subsided.

In this world we must expect suffering. Remember what Jesus said:

"Anyone who intends to come with me has to let me lead. You're not in the driver's seat—I am. Don't run from suffering; embrace it. Follow me and I'll show you how. Self-help is no help at all." (Luke 9:23-24, *The Message*)

As card-carrying members of the human race, we should expect suffering. Expect heartache. Expect pain and disappointment. Expect the unexpected. Yet while all this is true, we can also expect that as we give God the lead, He will give us what we need in order to endure the heartaches we experience. He will show us how to navigate the raging storms that come our way.

I recall taking our children to a pediatrician for checkups and being told that they needed immunizations. The nurse explained the risks and ramifications of the shots and quoted some statistics. One out of an astronomical number of children experiences adverse reactions, she said.

This information, I knew, was supposed to assure me that everything would be fine. But my mind went in another direction entirely. All I could think was that we had *already* defied the odds by having a child with Down's syndrome. Who was to say we wouldn't flout the odds again?

The trauma of a major disappointment or a painful loss tends to break down your defenses. You find it hard to expect much of anything for fear of being disappointed all over again. We went ahead with the shots...but not without anxiety.

In the midst of dealing with painful realities, relief can come as we revise our expectations to better fit our current situations. Remember: What is, is. To continue to hang on to expectations that are unsupported by the facts will simply intensify our struggle.

I can't expect life to be easy. But I can expect God to be who I need Him to be to me in the midst of my difficulties.

I can't expect myself to always be a wise, attentive, patient mom. I want to be, but so often I fail. I'm not always who or what I want to be. That's about the time I realize once again how profound and desperate my need is for God and His power to change me. That's when I have to hang on tightly to the expectation that the work He has started in me He will complete. That's when I must cling to the truth that His power in me "is able to carry out His purpose and do superabundantly, far over and above all that we dare ask or think—indefinitely beyond our highest prayers, desires, thoughts, hopes or dreams" (Ephesians 3:20, Amplified).

As I continue moving toward my tomorrows, my expectations will likely have to be revised now and then. When? Where? I don't know. But one thing I do know: In spite of the ups and downs and twists and turns that are yet ahead, God is able to get me to my final destination in glory.

And then every expectation I've ever had will fall absurdly short of reality.

Chapter Twenty-Eight

REFUSE TO ASSUME THE WORST

*Each of us makes his own weather,
and determines the color of the skies in the
emotional universe which he inhabits.*

FULTON J. SHEEN

Sometimes we frighten ourselves with our own thoughts. Our mind locks on an ordinary concern, stews on it a while, and then, before we know it, turns the problem into a horrible tragedy. In the counseling office we call this not-so-wonderful talent "catastrophizing."

After any situation in which our minds are overtaxed for a prolonged period of time, our psychological defenses are weak, and we find it difficult to ward off worries. Anxious thoughts that typically would bounce off of us during less stressful times seem to penetrate and stick. Once they stick, they grow, and we lose an accurate perception of what is really happening.

One of the best ways to manage worries that are multiplying exponentially is simply to interrupt the process in your head by saying firmly, "Stop it!" Assertively halt the escalating thoughts.

I remember well the week after I came home from the hospital following Nathan's birth. Grieving his Down syndrome and worried about the holes in his heart, I was in a dark funk. One afternoon John was home sick with the flu, and I was doing what I could to keep plenty of liquids and pain relievers handy for him. When I walked downstairs to our family room to give him some chicken noodle soup, I saw that he was sleeping.

I know this sounds a little strange, but something about the way he was lying there triggered my memory of seeing John's father in an open casket during his memorial service. Instantly, the thought shot through my mind: It's *probably some fatal illness, and John's going to die too*. Anxiety roared in my mind.

I shook my head in frustration, fully aware that the thought was irrational. "Stop it!" I blurted out. "This is ridiculous!"

My words startled John. In a flash he sat bolt upright and shouted, "What? What?"

His reaction scared me silly, and I screamed back, "What? What?"

And the soup? Well, let's just say it never made it to its intended destination.

We both burst out laughing when we realized what had happened. And you know what? When the gloomy thoughts stopped, my anxiety faded.

When we fuel our fears by catastrophizing, we actually create mental anguish and become our own worst enemy. The good news is that we don't have to compulsively follow every train of thought that enters our heads. A thought is simply a thought. We don't have to give it more power than it deserves.

In refusing to assume the worst, it helps if we give our scary predictions a reality check. I recently had a front-row seat watching Bill, a business executive, do this in the corporate world. After a number of his associates lost their positions due to a company merger, Bill made an appointment with me for some help in learning how to work with what he called "off-the-chart anxiety."

The last few months had been extremely stressful for those in the company's higher management positions. Bill wasn't sleeping well, and he felt as if he had to walk on pins and needles at the office. No one knew from one day to the next who might get the axe. Rumors flew. Some were founded on partial truth; others were gross exaggerations.

With the blood draining from his face, Bill told me, "I knew I was in trouble when my boss passed me in the hall and didn't even acknowledge me."

"Did he see you when you passed each other?" I asked.

"He couldn't have missed me," he replied. "There were just two of us in the hallway."

Bill went on to discuss some of the office politics involved and the reasons why he believed he would be laid off. "I think my boss is avoiding me because he knows I'm the next to go. I can feel it coming."

I do believe there are times when we can intuitively sense that something is coming down the pike, but my gut told me that Bill's anxiety, not the gift of discernment, was driving his impressions. His conclusion was natural for a mind riddled with worry.

Bill had not spoken to his boss since that troublesome day when they had silently passed each other in the hallway. I suggested that he test his fear against reality by scheduling an appointment with his boss as soon as possible. The unknowns were giving too much room for speculation. Bill's goal was to check out his impressions.

Two weeks later Bill returned. He'd had a long discussion with his boss about the company merger, and in that meeting he saw a whole new side of his boss. Clarity had come to him. When his boss identified Bill as "a key contributor with a bright future," Bill knew that his boss had confidence in him. He realized that his earlier impressions had been far off the mark. They were irrational fears fueled by the stressful changes on the job and his chronic fatigue.

When I asked Bill about the incident in the hallway, he shrugged it off, saying that his boss probably hadn't seen him because he was preoccupied. It was a healthy perspective coming from a peaceful mind.

When we're worried and anxious, our imaginations can run wild. And the more they do, the more anxious we feel. It's a vicious spiral. But the spiral can be easily interrupted. We can say "Stop" to our thoughts. We can test reality and refuse to let little things become big things. If you want to let go of worry and anxiety, remind yourself: *This problem doesn't have to be a big deal. I don't have to blow things out of proportion.*

A pebble is a pebble, not a boulder. A speed bump is a speed bump, not an impenetrable concrete wall. A concern is a concern, not a major disaster. A temporary setback is just that, not a permanent failure cast in stone for all of eternity.

Keep that in mind the next time you start to assume the worst— and let your anxiety go.

Chapter Twenty-Nine

REQUIRE
A PLAN

Four steps to achievement:
Plan purposefully, prepare prayerfully,
proceed positively, pursue persistently.

WILLIAM ARTHUR WARD

Worries and fears tend to jump-start the imagination into overdrive. Surprisingly, this typically occurs when the mind is quiet. You can disregard something that is bothering you through the course of a busy day, but once you settle down in the evening for some peace and quiet, those worrisome thoughts start intruding again. After a mostly worry-free, fully scheduled day and evening, you can fall into bed exhausted and go to sleep immediately only to have the anxieties show up in your dreams.

Why? Because worry tends to feed on a passive mind.

One of the best remedies for worry is to develop a plan of action *before* your imagination has an opportunity to be reactivated. Developing an advance plan can hold anxiety at bay. Just knowing that you're taking concrete steps to work on a problem can bring relief.

When Nathan was about four years old, we became aware of his marvelous (but hair-raising) sense of adventure. Every so often he threw us a curveball by leaving the house without telling us where he was going. We learned from other parents that this is a common occurrence among children with Down's syndrome. When these youngsters wander, they are simply following through with a fun idea that has come to mind. Because of their limited cognitive abilities, they don't sense the potential danger. Nathan had no idea that his escapes threw all of us into panic mode. He was just having a grand time exploring the world.

For our own peace of mind, we devised a plan. We secured extra bolts to the tops of all doors leading outside. We activated a beeper on our alarm system so we would know whenever a door was opened. We bought Nathan a new identification bracelet and necklace with his name, address, and phone number on them. Each family member agreed to keep a more watchful eye on him, and I even checked into using a local dog-search service in case an emergency occurred and the police weren't able to help. Finally, we consulted a developmental behavioral pediatrician for family counseling. We wanted to find ways to deal with the anxieties Nathan's escapes aroused in all of us. Each piece of our plan helped to increase our sense of control and decrease what we perceived as Nathan's vulnerability to danger.

The specialist we consulted gave us added insight. "The more children are hovered over, the more they'll bolt," he told us. "They'll react against boundaries that are too restricting." Because of his past escapades, we were afraid that Nathan would run off again, and we admitted that he probably sensed us hovering. The doctor suggested that we intentionally ease the restrictions and send him on small, safe, independent missions.

So we developed another plan. Instead of getting the mail ourselves, we asked Nathan to do it for us as we watched (out of Nathan's view) from a window. When he accomplished the task without bolting, we high-fived each other for a job well done. We also started asking him to let the dogs in and out and to help feed them their evening meal.

What the doctor said made sense. Our fear was constricting Nathan, and he was reacting against it. The more freedom we provided for him, the less he needed to push the limits. Developing a plan with the help of an expert made all the difference in the world. I've seen this work for others too.

I remember counseling Mark, a graduate student who suffered from severe anxiety before major exams. There was an interesting twist to this case: Mark's anxiety was not related to his test performance. This young man was an extremely intelligent, top-notch student who had a photographic memory. The college he attended was highly competitive, and his personal goal was to graduate at the top of his class. The cause of his anxiety was not the fear that he would do poorly on his exams; he was instead riddled with worry about not waking up in time to get to them.

In his first term at school he stayed up all night before tests to eliminate the possibility of missing them. That routine was killing him. I suggested that he develop a more realistic plan to reduce his anxiety.

A plan unfolded during the counseling session. Mark decided to set his wristwatch alarm to beep two hours before an exam. This gave him time to wake up, shower, and review his notes before the test. He also set the alarm on his clock radio to blare music full volume from the other side of the room so he had to get out of bed to turn it off. As an added precaution, he asked his roommate to rouse him just in case he slept through both alarms. Last but not least, he enlisted his best friend on campus to knock on his door an hour before the exam to make sure he was up and ready to go.

As you can imagine, the wristwatch alarm was enough to jolt

him out of his slumber, and he was on his feet in seconds. Anyone who is that conscientious about his studies isn't going to ignore an alarm. But before he went to bed at night his *imagination* wouldn't let him believe that one alarm was sufficient. To quiet it he had to develop what he considered to be a fail-safe plan. By the end of his second year of school, Mark's pre-exam anxieties were under control. The last I heard is that he is practicing with a prestigious law firm downtown and sleeping like a baby at night.

Formulating a plan doesn't have to take a lot of time or be a complicated process. It can be as simple as identifying a few specific steps you can take to increase your sense of control.

If you're worried about how you're going to pay your children's college tuitions, consult a financial advisor to devise a plan. Investigate the options with someone who can guide you in the process.

If you're worried about your child's academic performance, make a phone call. Connect with the counselors and teachers in the school system. Utilize their input and experience to form and implement a plan. The more support people you can include in the process, the more likely the plan will succeed.

If you're confused or don't know where to go for help in the planning process, ask God. He knows all the ins and outs of the situations that concern you, and He will give you wisdom. Nothing you are facing catches Him by surprise. He is able to lead, guide, and enlighten you about the next step to take. Ultimately, He is the One with all the answers.

With your highest welfare in mind, He can help you develop a plan. But that's not all. He'll also give you the power to achieve it.

Chapter Thirty

REASSURE
YOURSELF

God always gives us strength enough,
and sense enough, for everything He wants us to do.

JOHN RUSKIN

I have a question for you: What do you think is the most frequent instruction God gives to the human race?

What do you think?

Love one another?

Love God?

Pray?

Don't sin?

No, the most common instruction to men and women in all the
Bible is *"Don't be afraid!"* Three hundred sixty-five verses in the Bible
address our fears, anxieties, and worries. That's one golden nugget
for each day of the year. God knows our frailties. He understands our
tendency to fret, and time and again He offers us reassurance.

I've heard people say, "I wouldn't be so worried and anxious if I
didn't have this big problem." The underlying assumption is that *it's
the situation they're facing* that stokes their anxiety.

I'm not so sure.

If that's the case, why can two people in the same situation have totally different responses? Why does one person feel panic when another feels peace? Why do some exhibit worry, anxiety, and even terror, while others exude confidence and bold courage? Let's consider a couple of situations where we find opposite responses to the same threatening circumstances.

When Moses sent scouts to explore the Promised Land, he ordered twelve of his brightest and best-trained warriors to spy out the enemy territory and report back to him (Numbers 13–14). When they returned, ten of the scouts told Moses that the land was rich and fertile. Without a doubt, it was the best piece of real estate around. But they were terrified of the people who lived there. "They are too strong for us!" they cried. "They're giants! We are like grasshoppers compared to them! We'll never conquer them!"

But two of the soldiers, Joshua and Caleb, had a very different response. They looked at the same land, saw the same towering giants, and told Moses, "The land is awesome and our enemies are huge, but we will certainly conquer them with God's help."

Ten of the spies responded with panic, two with peace.

Then there's the well-known story of David and Goliath (1 Samuel 17). One afternoon, Jesse, David's father, called the young boy in from tending sheep and asked him to deliver some supplies to his brothers, who were serving in Israel's army. Toting a bundle of food under his arm, David made the trek to the Valley of Elah, where the Israelites were encamped on a hill opposite the army of the Philistines.

Every day, Goliath, the Philistines' champion, stood on the plain in the valley, mocking God and daring anyone from Israel's army to fight him. Every day for forty days no one had accepted his challenge. Everyone knew that it was a suicide mission. Goliath was too big, too formidable a foe.

It's no wonder. Goliath came from Gath, the part of the

Promised Land known as the "land of the giants" — the same region Moses' scouts had spied out. Of all the giants in the land, Goliath, who stood about nine feet seven inches tall, was the biggest of all. And his weapons were just as intimidating as his size. He carried a javelin as big as a weaver's beam, with an iron point that weighed about twenty-five pounds. His spear was like a small telephone pole with a twenty-five-pound, razor-sharp arrow on the end. His coat of armor weighed nearly two hundred pounds. Scholars have calculated that in order to be mobile while wearing this weighty armor, Goliath must have weighed between four hundred and five hundred pounds, with about one percent body fat.

When David walked into camp on the forty-first day, Goliath was in the middle of the field screaming blasphemies and strutting his seven hundred pounds of muscle and metal, while the Israelites stood motionless and terrified. Except David. He surprised everyone. He marched into the valley, pausing just long enough to pick up five stones and put one of them in his sling. Then he ran full speed ahead at Goliath. You know the rest of the story: With one little stone, David slew the giant.

Thousands of people lined both sides of the valley that day, and all they could see was Goliath. He was so big and so intimidating that they couldn't take their eyes off of him. David saw what everyone else saw that day, and yet he was fearless when others were shaking in their boots. What made the difference? What gave him confidence and courage?

David's words to Goliath reveal the source of the young man's strength:

> "You come against me with sword and spear and javelin, but
> I come against you in the name of the LORD Almighty, the
> God of the armies of Israel, whom you have defied. This day

the LORD will hand you over to me, and I'll strike you down and cut off your head.... And the whole world will know that there is a God in Israel. All those gathered here will know that it is not by sword or spear that the LORD saves; for the battle is the LORD's, and he will give all of you into our hands." (1 Samuel 17:45-47)

The first stone that David slung at Goliath was not one he picked up off the ground; it was the truth about God. David knew that God is all-powerful and that He was on his side. That truth steadied him. His confidence didn't come from analyzing, assessing, or running calculations. He didn't spend his mental energy on what ifs or evaluating whether or not he had the resources necessary to win the battle. His mind wasn't on any of those things. It was on God and His ability.[1]

When towering giants suddenly appear on the horizon of our lives, we, like David, need reassurance that God is mighty on our behalf. That means reminding ourselves that the same God who spoke the universe into existence can create something out of nothing in whatever problematic situation we're facing. It means reassuring ourselves that the same God whom David boasted of more than two thousand years ago is eager to help us slay the giants that have us shaking in our boots. One of the nicest gifts we can give ourselves when we're facing threatening situations is to remind ourselves that God is with us and that everything is going to be all right. When it's all said and done, He has the final say. This is not blind optimism, naïveté, or a Pollyanna approach to life. It's a fact, and it is based on the truth about God as He has revealed Himself to mankind.

May I offer you some truths to sling at your own personal giants? Try pulling a few of these stones out of your pocket the next time worry has you shaking in your boots.

- *"The LORD is close to the brokenhearted and saves those who are crushed in spirit" (Psalm 34:18).* When you feel defeated, beaten down by life, and worried that you don't have what it takes to endure, remember this truth: You may not have what you need, but God does, and He promises to stick close to your side and see you through. He will be your champion and companion in your suffering.

- *"The LORD will fight for you while you keep silent" (Exodus 14:14, NASB).* When you are treated unjustly or unfairly accused, God will be your defense. He will fight for you. Be still. Keep your mouth closed and your eyes open. Watch Him act on your behalf.

- *"Jesus...said, 'With man this is impossible, but with God all things are possible'" (Matthew 19:26).* When you see no way, God will make one. It's not up to you; it's up to Him.

- *"Even though I walk through the valley of the shadow of death, I will fear no evil, for you are with me.... Surely goodness and love will follow me all the days of my life"* (Psalm 23:4, 6). When you are riddled with worry or anxiety, you can reassure yourself that God is good. His goodness and love will continue to unfold in your life now and in the future.

- *"{Be} confident of this, that he who began a good work in you will carry it on to completion" (Philippians 1:6).* Even though you might not have a clue about what's going on in your life, God sees the whole picture. He knows what He is doing, and it's a good work. Be confident that He hasn't brought you this far just to leave you hanging. Reassure yourself that God will accomplish what concerns you.

- *"I will instruct you and teach you in the way you should go; I will counsel you and watch over you"* (Psalm 32:8). You have the wisest Guide in the universe to lead you. When you are worried about making a good decision, God will instruct you. He knows every pro and con of every option you're considering. Ask Him for wisdom. Reassure yourself that God always has your best interest at heart and that He will never steer you in a wrong direction.

- *"Now to him {God} who is able to do immeasurably more than all we ask or imagine, according to his power that is at work within us, to him be glory"* (Ephesians 3:20–21). You have never prayed a prayer that matches God's power. You have never asked for anything that has fully tapped God's capabilities. Let your imagination run wild with that idea for a moment. Then ask.

- *"But I trust in you, O LORD; I say, 'You are my God.' My times are in your hands"* (Psalm 31:14–15). When you're anxious about the timing of something important to you, reassure yourself that God is overseeing every detail of your life. He is never in a hurry and never late. Relax in His timing. Events will unfold according to His plan.

Confidence. Boldness. Courage. That sense of feeling released to bravely move forward. David had all those things when he squared off against Goliath in the Valley of Elah. They can be yours, too, when you reassure yourself with truth. Remember, your perspective determines whether you will experience panic or peace.

When you keep God in your sights, your courage soars. You can face your giants, and then let them go.

Reclaim Your Life

FOOD FOR THOUGHT

*Commit to the LORD whatever you do,
and your plans will succeed.*

PROVERBS 16:3

PRAYER FOR TODAY

Lord, my plate feels so full. So many things in my life have turned out differently than I expected, and I worry about things in the future. Please still my thoughts. Renew my mind to assume the best. Grant me wisdom to adjust my expectations. I want to prepare my spirit for the future that you have for me, one in which you promise that You are "able to do immeasurably more than all we ask or imagine, according to {Your} power that is at work within us." I cling to that promise now and wait expectantly for what is to come. In Your precious name, amen.

STEPS TO TAKE THIS MONTH

- What expectations are you holding on to with tightly clenched fists? Try writing them down on a piece of paper. Then, after asking God to help you revise it, tear up that piece of paper and scatter it to the wind.

- Make a conscious effort to stop yourself when your imagination begins to take you down *that* road again. Ask God to help you to refuse to assume the worst about whatever situations you are dealing with this month. When you succeed, don't forget to thank God for giving you the power and strength.

- How has making a plan helped you let go of worries in the past? What plan you make for today that will send some worries scurrying away *today*?

- Meditate on one of the verses listed on pages 229–230 the next time a situation arises that normally triggers anxiety in you. Remind yourself that God is very close and all powerful. He is committed to helping you slay the giants in your life.

STEP INTO A LIFE OF FREEDOM

◦⦁◦

As a man gets wiser he expects less,
and probably gets more than he expects.

JOSEPH FARRELL

Chapter Thirty-One

REFOCUS

As we begin to focus upon God, the things
of the spirit will take shape before our inner eyes.

A. W. TOZER

When we want to begin moving forward again, we need to check our focus. Ask yourself:

- Am I focusing on my losses, or on my gains?

- Am I staring at a closed door behind me, or getting ready to walk through a new door in front of me?

- Am I clinging to an ending, or preparing for a new beginning?

- Am I complaining about things I can't change, or am I changing the things I can?

When Nathan was born, cards and letters poured in from family and friends. They wanted so much to help and to share our grief. One letter enclosed a newspaper clipping that challenged me to open my heart to the new direction my life had taken. It helped me see that by focusing on what I didn't have instead of on what I did I was causing much of my own anguish.

The clipping was a little story penned years ago by Emily Perl

Kingley. Anticipating the birth of a baby, she wrote, is like planning a fabulous vacation. Then delivery day comes, the wheels of the jumbo jet touch down, and you awaken from your slumber to hear a flight attendant's cheery voice say, "Welcome to Holland."

"Holland!" you exclaim. "What do you mean *Holland?* I signed up for Italy! I'm supposed to be in Italy. All my life I've dreamed of going to Italy."

But there's been a change in the flight plan. They've landed in Holland and there you must stay.

The important thing is that they haven't taken you to a horrible, disgusting, filthy place, full of pestilence, famine, and disease. It's just a *different* place.

So you must go out and buy new guidebooks. And you must learn a whole new language. And you will meet a whole new group of people you would never have met.

It's just a different place. It's slower paced than Italy, less flashy than Italy. But after you've been there a while and you catch your breath, you look around, and you begin to notice that Holland has windmills. Holland has tulips. Holland even has Rembrandts.

But everyone you know is busy coming and going from Italy, and they're all bragging about what a wonderful time they had there. And for the rest of your life, you will say, "Yes, that's where I was supposed to go. That's what I had planned." And the pain of that will never, ever, ever go away, because the loss of that dream is a very significant loss. But if you spend your life mourning the fact that you didn't get to Italy, you may never be free to enjoy the special and very lovely things about Holland.[4]

Shifting our focus from what we don't have to what we do have brings a quiet calm to a heart torn with conflict. Peace comes when we make a simple choice to take a deep breath and say to ourselves, *I am exactly where I am supposed to be at this moment.* It means that we stop wasting precious time and emotional energy wishing things were different, longing to be someone else, or wanting another set of circumstances. Refocusing can lead us away from despair toward a greater sense of well-being as we trust that "my times are in Your hand" (Psalm 31:15, NKJV).

It doesn't matter what the circumstance is. It may be singleness or widowhood. It may be a heartbreaking marriage, infertility, disability, betrayal, a child gone astray, job loss, or a lingering illness. Whatever the life situation is in which we find ourselves with no control, we can refocus. With Paul we can learn to concentrate on "whatever is true, whatever is noble, whatever is right, whatever is pure, whatever is lovely, whatever is admirable...anything {that} is excellent or praiseworthy" (Philippians 4:8).

This mental discipline is part of the "secret" that Paul described a few verses later:

> I know what it is to be in need, and I know what it is to have plenty. I have learned the secret of being content in any and every situation.... I can do everything through him who gives me strength. (Philippians 4:12–13)

As life would have it, there will be many times when you and I will find ourselves in a "different place." That much is clear. But *God* will be with us in that different place. And as we open our hearts to Him, He will give us the strength we need to carry on. He will carry us through our disappointments and painful losses to a place of acceptance and peace.

That doesn't mean we won't feel sad now and then. We will.

That doesn't mean we won't play the "What if?" game. We will.

That doesn't mean we will never daydream about "Italy." We will.

But as time passes, we will do so less and less.

I am grateful that God has taught our family to perceive Nathan's differences as unique qualities to be appreciated and understood. I am grateful that the joy we feel over what Nathan can do far surpasses the sadness over what he cannot do. As time has passed, a shift in focus has enabled us to clearly see that there's a lot of love in Holland—but we had to let go of Italy to enjoy it.

Chapter Thirty-Two

REST IN GOD

O ne of the most difficult-to-handle aspects of letting go is time. Healing usually doesn't come all at once—and often it doesn't come as fast as we would like. When suffering lingers, we have moments when we wonder if we have what it takes to endure. We're not sure we can persevere through the pain. We glance behind us and see the looming disappointments. After a severe loss our psychological defenses are down, and we tend to forecast more gloom and doom. But morosely obsessing over the past or frantically fretting over the future does nothing to help us heal.

There's another way—a way that leads to rest. Centuries ago the prophet Isaiah wrote, "{God} will keep in perfect peace all those who trust in him, whose thoughts turn often to the Lord!" (Isaiah 26:3, TLB). Rest comes as we live in the moment—not in the past or the future—with an awareness that God loves us and wants to heal our anguish. As we let go of whatever we're squeezing in our relentless grip and simply trust Him, the empty spaces in our souls become the places God fills with the healing power of His presence.

Children have a knack for living in the present and trusting those who love them. They are less concerned about the cares of life, the worries of tomorrow, and the regrets or mistakes of the past. They simply give their full attention to the moment, to whatever they are doing, and enjoy it to the fullest.

It's amazing what kids can teach us about life. I want to close this book with a story that I have reflected on many times while facing the harsh realities of this world. It's a snapshot from a time in my life when I was deeply mourning the losses my little boy suffers because of Down's syndrome.

The Lord sometimes speaks to me in pictures. This was one of those occasions. One afternoon as I watched Nathan in physical therapy, God taught me a lesson about letting go and resting in Him.

Shortly after Nathan was born we enrolled him in an early intervention program in which therapists exercised his mind and body to enhance his development. When he was an infant, Nathan's interventions were one-on-one; but as a toddler he was moved into a classroom setting with several special-needs children.

During the first part of class the children met in a large, open room where a physical therapist led them in exercises designed to strengthen muscle tone and develop motor skills. Upbeat music filled the room while the children made their best efforts to accomplish simple toe touches, arm reaches, handclaps, bends, and stretches.

I recalled watching similar routines when Jessie and Ben were in preschool. "Head and shoulder, knees and toes," the kids had chimed along with the tape, keeping their motions in cadence with the music. Their movements jibed with the beat. Their actions were precise, clearly defined, and consistent. But Nathan's class was a much different picture. The children's motions were awkward and rarely in sync with the leader's. If one of the children happened to dance in rhythm, it was more often than not a happy accident.

But a day came when Nathan lit up with a sense of pride while delivering a perfect performance. He was in step with the therapist through the entire song. He didn't miss a beat. All his gestures were right on the mark.

It wasn't because John and I had practiced with him umpteen

times at home, and it wasn't because his muscle tone had miraculously changed from floppy to firm. On that particular day, Nathan had been selected for a demonstration. The therapist asked him to come to the front of the room and stand facing the class while she stood behind him.

"Nathan, lean back into me and put your hands in my hands," she instructed.

I watched Nathan relax his body into hers and place his little hands in her palms. When the music began, the therapist guided Nathan's arms through the routine. One, two, three, four. Up, down, all around. Together. Apart. Clap, clap, clap.

Nathan's droopy little arms did everything they were supposed to do as he let go and yielded to her lead. His assignment was to lean in and relax. The rest of the work was up to the therapist. Nathan's weakness was his greatest strength that day.

I embarrassed myself during that class. There we were in the middle of "up, down, clap, clap, clap," and I was wiping tears from my eyes. I secretly wondered if the other parents were thinking, *What's the big deal? She sure gets worked up over her son being picked to lead exercises!*

But it had nothing to do with what was going on inside me. The Lord was talking to me through my son. He showed me my need to lean back and rest in the safety of my Father's arms. He nudged me to let go of the things that were troubling me.

With a keen awareness of my own handicaps, I sensed the Lord reassuring me that His grace is sufficient for me. Should I lose my balance and stumble over bumps on my journey, God will steady me and hold me up. When I get out of step, He will help get me back in sync. The greater my weakness, the greater God's strength.

I don't have to be strong to be strong. Nor do you. And we can ease our pain by resting in the Lord…

…by living in the here and now,

…by leaning into God's sovereignty,

…by letting go and letting God take care of the rest.

As we learn to rest in God, time becomes our friend. As time passes we begin to experience spiritual and emotional healing.

One day we realize that we don't feel quite as much pain today as we did last week or last month. We laugh a little more, and the black cloud that comes and goes isn't quite as dark and doesn't hang around as long. We remember the pain, but it diminishes. We begin to realize that the days of mourning are giving way to newfound joys.

Letting go empowers transformation and releases us into freedom. Freedom does not mean we are able to do whatever we want to do. Freedom means we are released to become all that God wants us to be, to achieve all that God wants us to achieve, and to enjoy all that God wants us to enjoy.

God has given us a key role in experiencing and safeguarding our freedom of spirit, particularly when we are assaulted by harsh realities in this world. We must not allow our pain and struggle points to become the defining qualities of our lives. Quite the opposite. We must surrender everything to God and bank on the fact that in God's economy our losses become our gains. Disadvantages become advantages. When we entrust our *disappointments* into God's hands, they become His *appointments* for divine intervention. He does not allow the waves of grief washing over us to destroy us. Instead He uses them to redirect our lives.

Because of our belief in a home beyond this world, we can be realistic about the hardships that come our way without becoming

STEP TEN: STEP INTO A LIFE OF FREEDOM

hopeless. We don't have to get stuck in perpetual sorrow or bitter-ness. Grief has its proper place, but it is temporary—an episode in our journeys and not the whole story. Peter writes about the realities of our suffering in relation to eternity:

> What a God we have! And how fortunate we are to have him, this Father of our Master Jesus! Because Jesus was raised from the dead, we've been given a brand-new life and have everything to live for, including a future in heaven—and the future starts now! God is keeping careful watch over us and the future. The Day is coming when you'll have it all—life healed and whole.
> I know how great this makes you feel, even though you have to put up with every kind of aggravation in the meantime. (1 Peter 1:3–6, *The Message*)

Peter writes these words to encourage and strengthen the believers who were suffering persecution. They were enduring hardship in a society that brutally hated Christians. Peter was sensitive to this and spoke directly to their hearts, using the word *suffering* fifteen times in his book.

I love the way Peter validates their pain. He doesn't deny their suffering or minimize it. He doesn't gloss over it. He acknowledges it and in so many words says, " I know. I know it's hard...and God is with you and will bring you through. You will overcome. The same God who raised Jesus from the dead is the God who will bring you through. He will fortify your faith. God isn't going to let you down. Believe God. He will do what He says He will do."

And what does Peter say God is doing?

God is keeping careful watch over us and the future. The Day is coming when you'll have it all—life healed and whole. (1 Peter 1:5, *The Message*) Let me personalize this for you.

God is keeping careful watch over you and your future.

The words that Peter uses in the original language are full of pictures. Peter is saying, "God is keeping such careful watch over you that it's as if you are being shielded by him, with a host of militia guarding you in a fortress or a castle. He is watching every detail and shielding you. In the Spirit, you are in a fortified place. Not only is He keeping careful watch over you right now, but He also has an eye on your future, guarding what is rightfully yours in the days ahead."

You are being kept by the power of God. When Peter talks about the power of God, he's talking about the mighty miracle-working power of God he experienced firsthand. When Jesus intercepted people in their pain, Peter saw the blind receive their sight, the deaf hear, the dumb speak, the lame walk, and the lepers given fresh, new skin where limbs and flesh had been eaten away by disease.

Peter saw Jesus raise a young boy from the dead and feed five thousand from a few loaves and fishes. He was in the boat with twelve others who expected to die because the waves nearly flipped their tiny vessel when Jesus stilled the raging sea with a single word. This is the God who is keeping careful watch over you with a longing to restore you.

Peter tells us that we must not be surprised by suffering. It is part and parcel of living in a fallen world. Instead, be surprised by God's restoring power that springs forth from the depths of your pain.

God is mighty within you and is committed to restoring you.

He is on a mission to revive, refresh, and resurrect the dead places in your soul.

> "If you return to me, I will restore you...I will give you back your health and heal your wounds," says the LORD. (Jeremiah 15:19; 30:17, NLT)

To restore means to bring back to a former or original condition. When God restores, however, He goes beyond turning the clock back. Again and again in Scripture, we find that He always improves, increases, and multiplies something above and *beyond* its original condition. When God restored Job after the terrible trials he endured, He gave him twice what he had lost and blessed him more in his latter years of life than when he was in his prime (see Job 42:12–17). Jesus told his followers that if they suffered losses when following Him, He would restore their losses one hundred times over (Mark 10:29–30). God says, "If you return to me, I will restore you" (Jeremiah 15:19, NLT).

It's a beautiful promise. But there's a condition attached, isn't there?

If we return. *If* we do an about-face. *If* we abandon all of our self-redemptive strategies and begin moving toward God, He will restore us.

What does this mean, then? That we make a whole new sheet of resolutions or follow some kind of list full of rules or rituals? No. Our God's deepest desire is relationship with you and me. It is within a close personal connection with Him that the healing and rebuilding of our lives begins. It's in our dependence on Him that we are empowered to do the work of letting go.

Our job is to believe. God's job is to exert his miracle-working power. Our job is to place our faith in God. God's job is to find the answers, to bring the solutions, and to orchestrate our restoration.

When we come to the end of ourselves and open our hands, offering God all that we are and ever hope to be, we can trust that His healing will be progressive and continual. The healing process is kind of like peeling an onion. After we peel one layer, we become aware of something underneath that needs attention. With new awareness come fresh emotion and the need to face, embrace, and process the pain—and then let it go. In time we sense that new depth of character, emotional maturity, spiritual awakening, and newfound freedom in the wide open spaces of God's healing grace.

Jesus said:

"Are you tired? Worn out? Burned out on religion? Come to me. Get away with me and you'll recover your life. I'll show you how to take a real rest. Walk with me and work with me—watch how I do it. Learn the unforced rhythms of grace. I won't lay anything heavy or ill-fitting on you. Keep company with me and you'll learn to live *freely* and lightly." (Matthew 11:28–30, *The Message*)

Reclaim Your Life

FOOD FOR THOUGHT

For God is greater than our hearts, and he knows everything.

1 JOHN 3:20

PRAYER FOR TODAY

O Lord, when all is said and done, life boils down to believing You, loving You, and obeying You. I know I've been carrying weights that You never meant for me to carry and holding on to things that I need to release into Your hands. Dear Lord—You who love me so much—help me to trust You with all my heart. Help me to let go so that I can take Your hand and walk through life with You step by step, day by day. In Jesus' strong name I pray, amen.

STEPS TO TAKE THIS MONTH

- Has your plane to Italy ended up in Holland? What are some of the lovely things about your "Holland" that you can focus on?

- You don't have to be strong on your own. This month...

  ...live in the here and now.
  ...lean into God's sovereignty.
  ...let go and let God take care of the rest.

Rest in God and receive the power to let go...and step into a life of freedom.

NOTES

Chapter 1

1. Anne G. Perkins, "Medical Costs," *Harvard Business Review* 72, no. 6 (November/December 1994): 12.

2. Frank Minerth, Paul Meier, Don Hawkins, *Worry-Free Living* (Nashville, TN: Thomas Nelson Publishers, 1989), 17.

3. Martin Anthony, "Understanding Anxiety: Effects on Mental and Physical Health," symposium at Oregon Convention Center, 24 May 2001, Portland, Oregon.

Chapter 2

1. Billy Graham, *Billy Graham: The Inspirational Writings* (Dallas: Word, 1995).

2. Dr. Pamela Reeve, *Parables of the Forest* (Sisters, OR: Multnomah, 1989).

Chapter 10

1. Jean Lush and Pam Vredevelt, *Women and Stress* (Grand Rapids: Baker Books, 1992), 17.

Chapter 13

1. Questions adapted from Alan D. Wright, *The God Moment Principle* (Sisters, OR: Multnomah, 1999), 14.

Chapter 14

1. Robert Krant and Vicky Lundmark, "Internet Paradox: A Social Technology That Reduces Social Involvement and Psychological Well-Being?" *American Psychologist* 53, no. 9 (September 1998): 1017–1031.

Chapter 17

1. Dr. Theo Johnson, *Velvet Steel Anger Control Manual* (Gresham, OR: Healing Touch Ministries, 2000), 8. For more information, contact Dr. Johnson at www.healingtouchministries.org.

2. Dr. Willard Gaylan, *The Rage Within: Anger in Modern Life* (New York: Penguin Publishers, 1989), n.p.

Chapter 18

1. Dr. Albert Ellis, *Reason and Emotion in Psychotherapy* (New York: Carol Publishing Group, 1994), n.p.

Chapter 21

1. Dr. Ted Roberts, *Pure Desire* (Ventura, CA: Regal Books, 1999), 52.

2. Henri Nouwen, *The Road to Daybreak: A Spiritual Journey* (New York: Doubleday, 1988), 64–66.

Chapter 24

1. Brennan Manning, *Ruthless Trust: The Ragamuffin's Path to God* (San Francisco: HarperSanFrancisco, 2000), 96.

2. Matthew Henry's Commentary on Matthew 8:5–13 in The PC

Study Bible Complete Reference Library (Seattle: Biblesoft, 1992), 24.

3. Manning, *Ruthless Trust*, 11–12.

Chapter 25

1. Robert Bramson discusses these different types in *Coping with Difficult People* (New York: Ballantine, 1981).

2. Dr. Les Carter and Dr. Frank Minirth, *The Anger Workbook* (Nashville, TN: Thomas Nelson, 1993), 182.

Chapter 30

1. Dr. Mike Ladra, "Conquering Fear," adapted from a message given by the senior pastor at First Presbyterian Church, Salinas, California, 1999.

Chapter 31

1. Emily Perl Kingley, from an October 1992 "Dear Abby" column appearing in the *Oregonian*.

Hope and Healing
Are at Hand

"My pain is too deep for a Band-Aid."

"Will this heartache ever end?"

"Why me?"

Extraordinary emotional pain cries out for something more than a Band-Aid, a pat on the shoulder, or a greeting card cliché. When the wounds go deep, real help, honest encouragement, and tangible healing may be hard to locate.

Compassionate and experienced counselors Steve Stephens and Pam Vredevelt have walked alongside women in pain for years—they've heard the stories, seen the tears, felt the pain, and entered into the devastation. Real-life stories and proven, practical counsel serve as powerful tools to help you recover from past and present wounds, moving you into a new season of productive living.

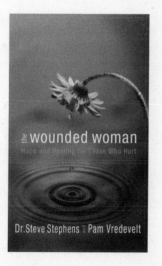

1-59052-529-9

visit www.mpbooks.com

Are you even thinking about walking out?

"I'm at the point where I don't think it is worth the effort anymore."

"The only reason I'm staying is because of the children."

"Surely God doesn't want me to be this unhappy."

Every woman longs to be appreciated, valued, and cared for. When these needs go unmet, she may be tempted to leave the husband she once loved—but walking out is seldom the path to happiness.

Like trusted friends, Dr. Steve Stephens and Alice Gray offer wise and gentle advice to restore hope to your marriage. You'll discover proven methods for how you can move toward each other rather than away, build up instead of tear down, and find love rather than lose it.

1-59052-267-2

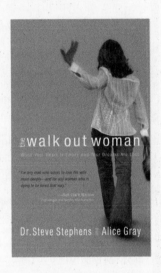

visit www.mpbooks.com | www.walkoutwoman.com

You've come a long way
...maybe.

"Most days I feel overwhelmed."

"I want to run away and start over."

"The joy and excitement are gone."

There are more than 60 million worn-out women in the U.S. today. If you're among them, this book will be like a retreat for your soul.

One short chapter at a time, you'll find simple steps to bring back the joy and energy of a rich life. What's more, you'll finally understand and learn to manage the sources of your exhaustion—perfectionism, guilt, unrealistic expectations, and difficult people—in a healthy way.

1-59052-266-4

visit www.mpbooks.com | www.multnomah.net/wornoutwoman

Also from
PAM VREDEVELT

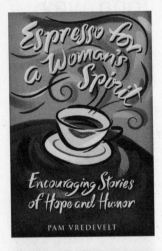

Espresso for
a Woman's Spirit

Need a spiritual lift? Drink in these true stories of God's miracles in the lives of ordinary women. You'll laugh. You'll cry. You'll declare, "Wow! God is awesome!"

1-57673-636-9

Espresso for
a Woman's Spirit,
Book 2

The way espresso jump-starts sluggish minds, *Espresso for a Woman's Spirit 2* energizes lagging spirits. Hilarious stories and poignant anecdotes fortify faith and lighten hearts.

1-57673-986-4

visit www.mpbooks.com | www.multnomah.net/vredevelt

PAM VREDEVELT

EMPTY ✤ ARMS

Hope and Support for Those Who

Have Suffered a Miscarriage, Stillbirth *or*

Tubal Pregnancy

1-57673-851-5

With the warmth and compassion of a licensed counselor and a Christian woman who has suffered miscarriage herself, Pam Vredevelt offers sound answers, advice, and reassurance to the woman fighting to maintain faith in this heartbreaking situation. *Empty Arms* is the essential guidebook through the agony of losing a child.

visit www.mpbooks.com I www.multnomah.net/vredevelt

Life-Changing Advice in a Quick-to-Read Format!

1-59052-432-2

1-59052-433-0

1-59052-434-9

1-59052-435-7

With sales of over 700,000 copies, the Lists to Live By series has something for everyone— guidance, inspiration, humor, family, love, health, and home. These books are perfect gift book for all occasions.

visit www.mpbooks.com I www.multnomah.net/liststoliveby